TEACHER'S PET PUBLICATIONS

PUZZLE PACK
for
Jacob Have I Loved

based on the book by
Katherine Paterson

Written by
Mary B. Collins

© 2005 Teacher's Pet Publications
All Rights Reserved

The materials in this packet are copyrighted
by Teacher's Pet Publications, Inc.

These pages may be duplicated by the purchaser
for use in the purchaser's own classroom.

Copying any of these materials and distributing them
for any other purpose is a violation of the copyright laws.

© 2005 Teacher's Pet Publications, Inc.
www.tpet.com

INTRODUCTION
If you already own the LitPlan for this title, this Puzzle Pack will refresh your Unit Resource Materials and Vocabulary Resource Materials sections plus give you additional materials you can substitute into the tests. If you do not already have a complete LitPlan, these pages will give you some supplemental materials to use with your own plan. There are two main groups of materials: one set for unit words (such as characters' names, symbols, places, etc.) and one set for vocabulary words associated with the book.

WORD LIST
There is a word list for both the unit words and the vocabulary words. These lists show you which words are being used in the materials and the clues or definitions being used for those words. You may want to give students a word list with clues/definitions to help them, or you may want students to only have a word list (without clues/definitions) if you want them to work a little harder. Both are available for duplication. The word lists can also be your "calling key" for the bingo games.

FILL IN THE BLANK AND MATCHING
There are 4 each of the fill in the blank and matching worksheets for both the unit and vocabulary words. These pages can be used either as extra worksheets for students or as objective parts of a unit test. They can be done individually if students need extra help or as a whole class activity to review the material covered.

MAGIC SQUARES
The magic squares not only reinforce the material covered but also work on reasoning and math skills. Many teachers have told us that their students really enjoy doing these!

WORD SEARCH PUZZLES
The word search words go in all directions, as indicated on your answer keys. Two of the word search puzzles have the clues listed rather than the words. This makes the puzzle a little more difficult, but it reinforces the material better. Two word search puzzles have words only for students who find the clue puzzles too difficult.

CROSSWORD PUZZLES
Both unit and vocabulary word sections have 4 crossword puzzles.

BINGO CARDS
There are 32 individual bingo cards for the unit words and 32 individual bingo cards for the vocabulary words. You can use your word list as a "call list," calling the words at random and marking them off of your list as you go, or you could use the flash cards by cutting them apart and drawing the words at random from a hat (or box or whatever). To make a better review, you might ask for the definition and spelling of each word as you call it out–or you could call out the definitions and have students tell you the words they need to look for on the puzzle.

JUGGLE LETTERS
The vocabulary juggle letter game is intended to help students learn the spellings of the words. One sheet has the definitions listed on it as an extra help for students who need it or to reinforce the definitions if you choose to do so.

FLASH CARDS
We've included a set of vocabulary flash cards you can duplicate, cut, and fold for your students. Some teachers make a few sets for general use by the class; others make a set for each student. Some teachers duplicate them for each student and have the students cut & fold their own. You can cut out just the words and put them in a hat, have each student pick out one word and write the definition and a sentence for that word. Students then swap words and papers, with the next student adding a sentence of his own under the last one. You can have students swap as many times as you like. Each time the student will read the sentences written prior to his own and then add a sentence. You can cut out the words and definitions separately and play "I Have; Who Has?" Each student in the room draws a word and definition. The first student says, "I have (the name of the word). Who has the definition?" The student with the definition reads it then says, "I have (the name of the vocabulary word she has). Who has the definition?" The round continues until all words and definitions have been given.

Jacob Have I Loved Word List

No.	Word	Clue/Definition
1.	BALTIMORE	Large Maryland seaport
2.	BLACKOUT	Darkened window coverings: ___ curtains
3.	BOHEME	Debuts Caroline as Musetta: La ___
4.	BOOMERANG	Came back every time the Australian threw it
5.	BRADSHAW	Waterman father of twins: Mr. ___
6.	BUSTER	Blue crab bursting out of its shell
7.	CALL	Mc___ Purnell
8.	CAPTAIN	Earned title of fifty year old waterman
9.	CAROLINE	Focal point of Mr. Rice's music program
10.	COUNTERSPY	Spies on another spy
11.	CRISFIELD	Maryland town closest to Rass by ferry
12.	CULLING	Sorting shellfish by size
13.	DREDGES	Large frames with nets used to collect shellfish
14.	EELGRASS	Marine plant with ribbon-like leaves
15.	ESAU	Swindled out of birthright by Biblical twin
16.	FDR	32nd President of the U.S.
17.	FERRY	Only island transportation
18.	GUNNYSACK	Bag used to put cats in
19.	GUT	Narrow channel of water
20.	HIRAM	Island native who returns after 50 years
21.	HITLER	Dictator of German Nazi party
22.	HURRICANE	It reduced island cat population by two-thirds.
23.	JACOB	Tricks blind father in Bible out of birthright
24.	JEAN	Betty ___ sings at the Christmas program.
25.	JERGENS	Gets thrown against a wall
26.	JIMMY	Male blue crab
27.	JOSEPH	Smiled like a man who would sing to the oysters
28.	JUILLIARD	New York City music conservatory
29.	KELLAMS	General store and post office on island
30.	KENTUCKY	Graduated a nurse-midwife from Rass
31.	LADIES	Women's group from church: ___ Society
32.	LEGACY	Fuel for scriptural quote by Grandma
33.	LOUISE	Cranky Grandma Bradshaw
34.	MAINLAND	Continental part of state
35.	MARYLAND	University Wheeze first attends
36.	MAST	Felled by Hiram Wallace during storm
37.	METHODISM	Island religion
38.	MIDWIFE	Delivers babies
39.	MOUNTAINS	Wheeze longs to see them.
40.	NIGHT	Sung by Betty Jean Boyd: O Holy ___
41.	OYSTER	Shells on island streets
42.	PACIFIC	Three island boys aboard the same ship died there: South ___
43.	PAREGORIC	Household remedy made from opium
44.	PARIS	Place Susan wanted to go to write poetry
45.	PATERSON	Author
46.	PEABODY	Baltimore music school
47.	PEARL	Naval base in Hawaii bombed by Japanese: ___ Harbor
48.	PERISCOPE	Used by the Captain to view Call and Wheeze
49.	PIANO	Instrument owned only by Bradshaws on island
50.	POKER	Wheeze beats Caroline satisfactorily at it
51.	PROG	To fish for crab

Jacob Have I Loved Word List Continued

No.	Word	Clue/Definition
52.	RANK	Blue crab ready to shed its shell: ___ peeler
53.	RASS	Chesapeake island near Crisfield
54.	RICE	He has a fiance in Baltimore.
55.	SABBATH	Holy day
56.	SALISBURY	Inland Eastern Shore Maryland town
57.	SEARS	Store where islanders order shoes
58.	SHADOW	Knows what evil lurks in the hearts of men: The ___
59.	SHANTY	Crab shack
60.	SKIFF	Wheeze's crabbing boat
61.	SKIPJACK	Waterman's vessel
62.	SOOK	Lady crab
63.	SPCA	Where Wheeze wants to take the cats
64.	SUN	Baltimore newspaper Wheeze reads
65.	SUSAN	Came to Rass to teach
66.	TIME	Source of Wheeze's jokes
67.	TONGS	Fork-like device used to retrieve oysters
68.	TRUDY	Woman Hiram marries
69.	TRUITT	Mountain-locked Appalachian valley
70.	UNLIMITED	Lyrics ___ misspelled Wheeze's name on form letter
71.	WATERMEN	They work on the water.
72.	WHEEZE	Sara Louise's nickname
73.	WONDER	Caroline's Christmas solo: I ___ As I ___

Jacob Have I Loved Fill In The Blanks 1

_____ 1. It reduced island cat population by two-thirds.

_____ 2. Gets thrown against a wall

_____ 3. Dictator of German Nazi party

_____ 4. Holy day

_____ 5. Delivers babies

_____ 6. Waterman father of twins: Mr. ___

_____ 7. Bag used to put cats in

_____ 8. Darkened window coverings: ___ curtains

_____ 9. Felled by Hiram Wallace during storm

_____ 10. Only island transportation

_____ 11. University Wheeze first attends

_____ 12. Lady crab

_____ 13. Blue crab ready to shed its shell: ___ peeler

_____ 14. Inland Eastern Shore Maryland town

_____ 15. General store and post office on island

_____ 16. To fish for crab

_____ 17. Chesapeake island near Crisfield

_____ 18. 32nd President of the U.S.

_____ 19. Sorting shellfish by size

_____ 20. Spies on another spy

Jacob Have I Loved Fill In The Blanks 1 Answer Key

HURRICANE	1. It reduced island cat population by two-thirds.
JERGENS	2. Gets thrown against a wall
HITLER	3. Dictator of German Nazi party
SABBATH	4. Holy day
MIDWIFE	5. Delivers babies
BRADSHAW	6. Waterman father of twins: Mr. ___
GUNNYSACK	7. Bag used to put cats in
BLACKOUT	8. Darkened window coverings: ___ curtains
MAST	9. Felled by Hiram Wallace during storm
FERRY	10. Only island transportation
MARYLAND	11. University Wheeze first attends
SOOK	12. Lady crab
RANK	13. Blue crab ready to shed its shell: ___ peeler
SALISBURY	14. Inland Eastern Shore Maryland town
KELLAMS	15. General store and post office on island
PROG	16. To fish for crab
RASS	17. Chesapeake island near Crisfield
FDR	18. 32nd President of the U.S.
CULLING	19. Sorting shellfish by size
COUNTERSPY	20. Spies on another spy

Jacob Have I Loved Fill In The Blanks 2

_____ 1. Graduated a nurse-midwife from Rass
_____ 2. Earned title of fifty year old waterman
_____ 3. Betty ___ sings at the Christmas program.
_____ 4. Sorting shellfish by size
_____ 5. Lady crab
_____ 6. He has a fiance in Baltimore.
_____ 7. Wheeze beats Caroline satisfactorily at it
_____ 8. Tricks blind father in Bible out of birthright
_____ 9. Naval base in Hawaii bombed by Japanese: ___ Harbor
_____ 10. New York City music conservatory
_____ 11. Chesapeake island near Crisfield
_____ 12. Wheeze longs to see them.
_____ 13. Source of Wheeze's jokes
_____ 14. Marine plant with ribbon-like leaves
_____ 15. Spies on another spy
_____ 16. Crab shack
_____ 17. General store and post office on island
_____ 18. Fuel for scriptural quote by Grandma
_____ 19. Baltimore newspaper Wheeze reads
_____ 20. Mc____ Purnell

Jacob Have I Loved Fill In The Blanks 2 Answer Key

KENTUCKY	1. Graduated a nurse-midwife from Rass
CAPTAIN	2. Earned title of fifty year old waterman
JEAN	3. Betty ___ sings at the Christmas program.
CULLING	4. Sorting shellfish by size
SOOK	5. Lady crab
RICE	6. He has a fiance in Baltimore.
POKER	7. Wheeze beats Caroline satisfactorily at it
JACOB	8. Tricks blind father in Bible out of birthright
PEARL	9. Naval base in Hawaii bombed by Japanese: ___ Harbor
JUILLIARD	10. New York City music conservatory
RASS	11. Chesapeake island near Crisfield
MOUNTAINS	12. Wheeze longs to see them.
TIME	13. Source of Wheeze's jokes
EELGRASS	14. Marine plant with ribbon-like leaves
COUNTERSPY	15. Spies on another spy
SHANTY	16. Crab shack
KELLAMS	17. General store and post office on island
LEGACY	18. Fuel for scriptural quote by Grandma
SUN	19. Baltimore newspaper Wheeze reads
CALL	20. Mc____ Purnell

Jacob Have I Loved Fill In The Blanks 3

_____ 1. Large frames with nets used to collect shellfish
_____ 2. Caroline's Christmas solo: I ___ As I ___
_____ 3. Baltimore music school
_____ 4. Author
_____ 5. Cranky Grandma Bradshaw
_____ 6. Gets thrown against a wall
_____ 7. Knows what evil lurks in the hearts of men: The ___
_____ 8. 32nd President of the U.S.
_____ 9. Where Wheeze wants to take the cats
_____ 10. Three island boys aboard the same ship died there: South____
_____ 11. Shells on island streets
_____ 12. Smiled like a man who would sing to the oysters
_____ 13. Swindled out of birthright by Biblical twin
_____ 14. Blue crab bursting out of its shell
_____ 15. Tricks blind father in Bible out of birthright
_____ 16. Island native who returns after 50 years
_____ 17. Marine plant with ribbon-like leaves
_____ 18. Sorting shellfish by size
_____ 19. Island religion
_____ 20. Came to Rass to teach

Jacob Have I Loved Fill In The Blanks 3 Answer Key

DREDGES	1. Large frames with nets used to collect shellfish
WONDER	2. Caroline's Christmas solo: I ___ As I ___
PEABODY	3. Baltimore music school
PATERSON	4. Author
LOUISE	5. Cranky Grandma Bradshaw
JERGENS	6. Gets thrown against a wall
SHADOW	7. Knows what evil lurks in the hearts of men: The ___
FDR	8. 32nd President of the U.S.
SPCA	9. Where Wheeze wants to take the cats
PACIFIC	10. Three island boys aboard the same ship died there: South____
OYSTER	11. Shells on island streets
JOSEPH	12. Smiled like a man who would sing to the oysters
ESAU	13. Swindled out of birthright by Biblical twin
BUSTER	14. Blue crab bursting out of its shell
JACOB	15. Tricks blind father in Bible out of birthright
HIRAM	16. Island native who returns after 50 years
EELGRASS	17. Marine plant with ribbon-like leaves
CULLING	18. Sorting shellfish by size
METHODISM	19. Island religion
SUSAN	20. Came to Rass to teach

Jacob Have I Loved Fill In The Blanks 4

_____   1. Chesapeake island near Crisfield
_____   2. Naval base in Hawaii bombed by Japanese: ___ Harbor
_____   3. Maryland town closest to Rass by ferry
_____   4. It reduced island cat population by two-thirds.
_____   5. Sara Louise's nickname
_____   6. To fish for crab
_____   7. They work on the water.
_____   8. Male blue crab
_____   9. Only island transportation
_____   10. Delivers babies
_____   11. Sorting shellfish by size
_____   12. Debuts Caroline as Musetta: La ___
_____   13. Household remedy made from opium
_____   14. Wheeze beats Caroline satisfactorily at it
_____   15. Lyrics ___ misspelled Wheeze's name on form letter
_____   16. Sung by Betty Jean Boyd: O Holy ___
_____   17. Focal point of Mr. Rice's music program
_____   18. Tricks blind father in Bible out of birthright
_____   19. Spies on another spy
_____   20. Darkened window coverings: ___ curtains

Jacob Have I Loved Fill In The Blanks 4 Answer Key

RASS	1. Chesapeake island near Crisfield
PEARL	2. Naval base in Hawaii bombed by Japanese: ___ Harbor
CRISFIELD	3. Maryland town closest to Rass by ferry
HURRICANE	4. It reduced island cat population by two-thirds.
WHEEZE	5. Sara Louise's nickname
PROG	6. To fish for crab
WATERMEN	7. They work on the water.
JIMMY	8. Male blue crab
FERRY	9. Only island transportation
MIDWIFE	10. Delivers babies
CULLING	11. Sorting shellfish by size
BOHEME	12. Debuts Caroline as Musetta: La ___
PAREGORIC	13. Household remedy made from opium
POKER	14. Wheeze beats Caroline satisfactorily at it
UNLIMITED	15. Lyrics ___ misspelled Wheeze's name on form letter
NIGHT	16. Sung by Betty Jean Boyd: O Holy ___
CAROLINE	17. Focal point of Mr. Rice's music program
JACOB	18. Tricks blind father in Bible out of birthright
COUNTERSPY	19. Spies on another spy
BLACKOUT	20. Darkened window coverings: ___ curtains

Jacob Have I Loved Matching 1

___ 1. GUNNYSACK   A. Inland Eastern Shore Maryland town
___ 2. LOUISE   B. Betty ___ sings at the Christmas program.
___ 3. SUN   C. Sung by Betty Jean Boyd: O Holy ___
___ 4. PIANO   D. Island native who returns after 50 years
___ 5. NIGHT   E. Tricks blind father in Bible out of birthright
___ 6. JEAN   F. University Wheeze first attends
___ 7. GUT   G. Wheeze longs to see them.
___ 8. WONDER   H. Caroline's Christmas solo: I ___ As I ___
___ 9. LEGACY   I. Island religion
___ 10. JACOB   J. Fuel for scriptural quote by Grandma
___ 11. BLACKOUT   K. Cranky Grandma Bradshaw
___ 12. METHODISM   L. Came back every time the Australian threw it
___ 13. WATERMEN   M. He has a fiance in Baltimore.
___ 14. HIRAM   N. Narrow channel of water
___ 15. SALISBURY   O. Darkened window coverings: ___ curtains
___ 16. RICE   P. Spies on another spy
___ 17. MARYLAND   Q. Instrument owned only by Bradshaws on island
___ 18. KELLAMS   R. It reduced island cat population by two-thirds.
___ 19. EELGRASS   S. They work on the water.
___ 20. MOUNTAINS   T. Dictator of German Nazi party
___ 21. MAST   U. Felled by Hiram Wallace during storm
___ 22. BOOMERANG   V. Marine plant with ribbon-like leaves
___ 23. HURRICANE   W. Bag used to put cats in
___ 24. COUNTERSPY   X. Baltimore newspaper Wheeze reads
___ 25. HITLER   Y. General store and post office on island

Jacob Have I Loved Matching 1 Answer Key

W - 1.	GUNNYSACK	A.	Inland Eastern Shore Maryland town
K - 2.	LOUISE	B.	Betty ___ sings at the Christmas program.
X - 3.	SUN	C.	Sung by Betty Jean Boyd: O Holy ___
Q - 4.	PIANO	D.	Island native who returns after 50 years
C - 5.	NIGHT	E.	Tricks blind father in Bible out of birthright
B - 6.	JEAN	F.	University Wheeze first attends
N - 7.	GUT	G.	Wheeze longs to see them.
H - 8.	WONDER	H.	Caroline's Christmas solo: I ___ As I ___
J - 9.	LEGACY	I.	Island religion
E - 10.	JACOB	J.	Fuel for scriptural quote by Grandma
O - 11.	BLACKOUT	K.	Cranky Grandma Bradshaw
I - 12.	METHODISM	L.	Came back every time the Australian threw it
S - 13.	WATERMEN	M.	He has a fiance in Baltimore.
D - 14.	HIRAM	N.	Narrow channel of water
A - 15.	SALISBURY	O.	Darkened window coverings: ___ curtains
M - 16.	RICE	P.	Spies on another spy
F - 17.	MARYLAND	Q.	Instrument owned only by Bradshaws on island
Y - 18.	KELLAMS	R.	It reduced island cat population by two-thirds.
V - 19.	EELGRASS	S.	They work on the water.
G - 20.	MOUNTAINS	T.	Dictator of German Nazi party
U - 21.	MAST	U.	Felled by Hiram Wallace during storm
L - 22.	BOOMERANG	V.	Marine plant with ribbon-like leaves
R - 23.	HURRICANE	W.	Bag used to put cats in
P - 24.	COUNTERSPY	X.	Baltimore newspaper Wheeze reads
T - 25.	HITLER	Y.	General store and post office on island

Copyrighted

Jacob Have I Loved Matching 2

___ 1. RANK   A. Wheeze longs to see them.
___ 2. EELGRASS   B. Came back every time the Australian threw it
___ 3. BUSTER   C. Came to Rass to teach
___ 4. TRUITT   D. University Wheeze first attends
___ 5. SHANTY   E. Swindled out of birthright by Biblical twin
___ 6. SKIPJACK   F. Three island boys aboard the same ship died there: South ___
___ 7. HITLER   G. Focal point of Mr. Rice's music program
___ 8. CAROLINE   H. Marine plant with ribbon-like leaves
___ 9. MOUNTAINS   I. Chesapeake island near Crisfield
___10. BLACKOUT   J. Blue crab bursting out of its shell
___11. BOOMERANG   K. It reduced island cat population by two-thirds.
___12. PAREGORIC   L. Mountain-locked Appalachian valley
___13. WHEEZE   M. Household remedy made from opium
___14. RASS   N. Sara Louise's nickname
___15. PARIS   O. Cranky Grandma Bradshaw
___16. HURRICANE   P. Crab shack
___17. TRUDY   Q. Holy day
___18. PACIFIC   R. Woman Hiram marries
___19. MARYLAND   S. Place Susan wanted to go to write poetry
___20. LOUISE   T. Darkened window coverings: ___ curtains
___21. SUSAN   U. Bag used to put cats in
___22. GUNNYSACK   V. Waterman's vessel
___23. SABBATH   W. Where Wheeze wants to take the cats
___24. ESAU   X. Blue crab ready to shed its shell: ___ peeler
___25. SPCA   Y. Dictator of German Nazi party

Jacob Have I Loved Matching 2 Answer Key

X - 1. RANK	A. Wheeze longs to see them.
H - 2. EELGRASS	B. Came back every time the Australian threw it
J - 3. BUSTER	C. Came to Rass to teach
L - 4. TRUITT	D. University Wheeze first attends
P - 5. SHANTY	E. Swindled out of birthright by Biblical twin
V - 6. SKIPJACK	F. Three island boys aboard the same ship died there: South ___
Y - 7. HITLER	G. Focal point of Mr. Rice's music program
G - 8. CAROLINE	H. Marine plant with ribbon-like leaves
A - 9. MOUNTAINS	I. Chesapeake island near Crisfield
T - 10. BLACKOUT	J. Blue crab bursting out of its shell
B - 11. BOOMERANG	K. It reduced island cat population by two-thirds.
M - 12. PAREGORIC	L. Mountain-locked Appalachian valley
N - 13. WHEEZE	M. Household remedy made from opium
I - 14. RASS	N. Sara Louise's nickname
S - 15. PARIS	O. Cranky Grandma Bradshaw
K - 16. HURRICANE	P. Crab shack
R - 17. TRUDY	Q. Holy day
F - 18. PACIFIC	R. Woman Hiram marries
D - 19. MARYLAND	S. Place Susan wanted to go to write poetry
O - 20. LOUISE	T. Darkened window coverings: ___ curtains
C - 21. SUSAN	U. Bag used to put cats in
U - 22. GUNNYSACK	V. Waterman's vessel
Q - 23. SABBATH	W. Where Wheeze wants to take the cats
E - 24. ESAU	X. Blue crab ready to shed its shell: ___ peeler
W - 25. SPCA	Y. Dictator of German Nazi party

Jacob Have I Loved Matching 3

___ 1. OYSTER A. Shells on island streets
___ 2. PERISCOPE B. Delivers babies
___ 3. KELLAMS C. Only island transportation
___ 4. PACIFIC D. Swindled out of birthright by Biblical twin
___ 5. SALISBURY E. Spies on another spy
___ 6. SPCA F. Island native who returns after 50 years
___ 7. LADIES G. Lyrics ___ misspelled Wheeze's name on form letter
___ 8. MIDWIFE H. Betty ___ sings at the Christmas program.
___ 9. PEARL I. Blue crab bursting out of its shell
___10. GUT J. Cranky Grandma Bradshaw
___11. ESAU K. Male blue crab
___12. LOUISE L. Used by the Captain to view Call and Wheeze
___13. JIMMY M. Holy day
___14. WHEEZE N. They work on the water.
___15. UNLIMITED O. Women's group from church: ___ Society
___16. SABBATH P. Sara Louise's nickname
___17. WATERMEN Q. Wheeze beats Caroline satisfactorily at it
___18. JACOB R. Tricks blind father in Bible out of birthright
___19. BUSTER S. Three island boys aboard the same ship died there: South ___
___20. TRUITT T. Mountain-locked Appalachian valley
___21. FERRY U. Inland Eastern Shore Maryland town
___22. COUNTERSPY V. Where Wheeze wants to take the cats
___23. JEAN W. Narrow channel of water
___24. HIRAM X. General store and post office on island
___25. POKER Y. Naval base in Hawaii bombed by Japanese: ___ Harbor

Jacob Have I Loved Matching 3 Answer Key

A - 1. OYSTER	A.	Shells on island streets
L - 2. PERISCOPE	B.	Delivers babies
X - 3. KELLAMS	C.	Only island transportation
S - 4. PACIFIC	D.	Swindled out of birthright by Biblical twin
U - 5. SALISBURY	E.	Spies on another spy
V - 6. SPCA	F.	Island native who returns after 50 years
O - 7. LADIES	G.	Lyrics ___ misspelled Wheeze's name on form letter
B - 8. MIDWIFE	H.	Betty ___ sings at the Christmas program.
Y - 9. PEARL	I.	Blue crab bursting out of its shell
W - 10. GUT	J.	Cranky Grandma Bradshaw
D - 11. ESAU	K.	Male blue crab
J - 12. LOUISE	L.	Used by the Captain to view Call and Wheeze
K - 13. JIMMY	M.	Holy day
P - 14. WHEEZE	N.	They work on the water.
G - 15. UNLIMITED	O.	Women's group from church: ___ Society
M - 16. SABBATH	P.	Sara Louise's nickname
N - 17. WATERMEN	Q.	Wheeze beats Caroline satisfactorily at it
R - 18. JACOB	R.	Tricks blind father in Bible out of birthright
I - 19. BUSTER	S.	Three island boys aboard the same ship died there: South ___
T - 20. TRUITT	T.	Mountain-locked Appalachian valley
C - 21. FERRY	U.	Inland Eastern Shore Maryland town
E - 22. COUNTERSPY	V.	Where Wheeze wants to take the cats
H - 23. JEAN	W.	Narrow channel of water
F - 24. HIRAM	X.	General store and post office on island
Q - 25. POKER	Y.	Naval base in Hawaii bombed by Japanese: ___ Harbor

Copyrighted

Jacob Have I Loved Matching 4

___ 1. BLACKOUT A. Wheeze's crabbing boat
___ 2. SALISBURY B. Instrument owned only by Bradshaws on island
___ 3. BUSTER C. Blue crab bursting out of its shell
___ 4. UNLIMITED D. Shells on island streets
___ 5. SKIPJACK E. Wheeze longs to see them.
___ 6. CAPTAIN F. Women's group from church: ___ Society
___ 7. LADIES G. Knows what evil lurks in the hearts of men: The ___
___ 8. MOUNTAINS H. Large frames with nets used to collect shellfish
___ 9. BOHEME I. Holy day
___ 10. HIRAM J. Earned title of fifty year old waterman
___ 11. KENTUCKY K. Sara Louise's nickname
___ 12. OYSTER L. Graduated a nurse-midwife from Rass
___ 13. TRUDY M. Waterman's vessel
___ 14. WHEEZE N. Cranky Grandma Bradshaw
___ 15. LOUISE O. Felled by Hiram Wallace during storm
___ 16. PERISCOPE P. Bag used to put cats in
___ 17. SHANTY Q. Debuts Caroline as Musetta: La ___
___ 18. SHADOW R. Inland Eastern Shore Maryland town
___ 19. PIANO S. Used by the Captain to view Call and Wheeze
___ 20. MAST T. Woman Hiram marries
___ 21. SKIFF U. Lyrics ___ misspelled Wheeze's name on form letter
___ 22. GUNNYSACK V. Large Maryland seaport
___ 23. SABBATH W. Darkened window coverings: ___ curtains
___ 24. DREDGES X. Crab shack
___ 25. BALTIMORE Y. Island native who returns after 50 years

Jacob Have I Loved Matching 4 Answer Key

W - 1. BLACKOUT	A.	Wheeze's crabbing boat
R - 2. SALISBURY	B.	Instrument owned only by Bradshaws on island
C - 3. BUSTER	C.	Blue crab bursting out of its shell
U - 4. UNLIMITED	D.	Shells on island streets
M - 5. SKIPJACK	E.	Wheeze longs to see them.
J - 6. CAPTAIN	F.	Women's group from church: ___ Society
F - 7. LADIES	G.	Knows what evil lurks in the hearts of men: The ___
E - 8. MOUNTAINS	H.	Large frames with nets used to collect shellfish
Q - 9. BOHEME	I.	Holy day
Y - 10. HIRAM	J.	Earned title of fifty year old waterman
L - 11. KENTUCKY	K.	Sara Louise's nickname
D - 12. OYSTER	L.	Graduated a nurse-midwife from Rass
T - 13. TRUDY	M.	Waterman's vessel
K - 14. WHEEZE	N.	Cranky Grandma Bradshaw
N - 15. LOUISE	O.	Felled by Hiram Wallace during storm
S - 16. PERISCOPE	P.	Bag used to put cats in
X - 17. SHANTY	Q.	Debuts Caroline as Musetta: La ___
G - 18. SHADOW	R.	Inland Eastern Shore Maryland town
B - 19. PIANO	S.	Used by the Captain to view Call and Wheeze
O - 20. MAST	T.	Woman Hiram marries
A - 21. SKIFF	U.	Lyrics ___ misspelled Wheeze's name on form letter
P - 22. GUNNYSACK	V.	Large Maryland seaport
I - 23. SABBATH	W.	Darkened window coverings: ___ curtains
H - 24. DREDGES	X.	Crab shack
V - 25. BALTIMORE	Y.	Island native who returns after 50 years

Jacob Have I Loved Magic Squares 1

Match the definition with the vocabulary word. Put your answers in the magic squares below. When your answers are correct, all columns and rows will add to the same number.

A. HIRAM
B. LOUISE
C. BLACKOUT
D. SUN

E. RICE
F. TRUDY
G. SABBATH
H. JOSEPH

I. MARYLAND
J. SHANTY
K. SPCA
L. MAST

M. WONDER
N. PEABODY
O. POKER
P. SOOK

1. Darkened window coverings: ___ curtains
2. Crab shack
3. Woman Hiram marries
4. Wheeze beats Caroline satisfactorily at it
5. Lady crab
6. He has a fiance in Baltimore.
7. University Wheeze first attends
8. Baltimore newspaper Wheeze reads
9. Caroline's Christmas solo: I ___ As I ___
10. Smiled like a man who would sing to the oysters
11. Felled by Hiram Wallace during storm
12. Island native who returns after 50 years
13. Cranky Grandma Bradshaw
14. Where Wheeze wants to take the cats
15. Holy day
16. Baltimore music school

A=	B=	C=	D=
E=	F=	G=	H=
I=	J=	K=	L=
M=	N=	O=	P=

22
Copyrighted

Jacob Have I Loved Magic Squares 1 Answer Key

Match the definition with the vocabulary word. Put your answers in the magic squares below. When your answers are correct, all columns and rows will add to the same number.

A. HIRAM
B. LOUISE
C. BLACKOUT
D. SUN

E. RICE
F. TRUDY
G. SABBATH
H. JOSEPH

I. MARYLAND
J. SHANTY
K. SPCA
L. MAST

M. WONDER
N. PEABODY
O. POKER
P. SOOK

1. Darkened window coverings: ___ curtains
2. Crab shack
3. Woman Hiram marries
4. Wheeze beats Caroline satisfactorily at it
5. Lady crab
6. He has a fiance in Baltimore.
7. University Wheeze first attends
8. Baltimore newspaper Wheeze reads
9. Caroline's Christmas solo: I ___ As I ___
10. Smiled like a man who would sing to the oysters
11. Felled by Hiram Wallace during storm
12. Island native who returns after 50 years
13. Cranky Grandma Bradshaw
14. Where Wheeze wants to take the cats
15. Holy day
16. Baltimore music school

A=12	B=13	C=1	D=8
E=6	F=3	G=15	H=10
I=7	J=2	K=14	L=11
M=9	N=16	O=4	P=5

Jacob Have I Loved Magic Squares 2

Match the definition with the vocabulary word. Put your answers in the magic squares below. When your answers are correct, all columns and rows will add to the same number.

A. BUSTER
B. MAST
C. PEARL
D. JOSEPH
E. BOHEME
F. PATERSON
G. SKIFF
H. WATERMEN
I. TONGS
J. SUN
K. GUNNYSACK
L. GUT
M. PAREGORIC
N. FERRY
O. MIDWIFE
P. TIME

1. Felled by Hiram Wallace during storm
2. Wheeze's crabbing boat
3. Bag used to put cats in
4. Only island transportation
5. Household remedy made from opium
6. Narrow channel of water
7. They work on the water.
8. Blue crab bursting out of its shell
9. Source of Wheeze's jokes
10. Fork-like device used to retrieve oysters
11. Debuts Caroline as Musetta: La ___
12. Smiled like a man who would sing to the oysters
13. Naval base in Hawaii bombed by Japanese: ___ Harbor
14. Author
15. Baltimore newspaper Wheeze reads
16. Delivers babies

A=	B=	C=	D=
E=	F=	G=	H=
I=	J=	K=	L=
M=	N=	O=	P=

Jacob Have I Loved Magic Squares 2 Answer Key

Match the definition with the vocabulary word. Put your answers in the magic squares below. When your answers are correct, all columns and rows will add to the same number.

A. BUSTER
B. MAST
C. PEARL
D. JOSEPH
E. BOHEME
F. PATERSON
G. SKIFF
H. WATERMEN
I. TONGS
J. SUN
K. GUNNYSACK
L. GUT
M. PAREGORIC
N. FERRY
O. MIDWIFE
P. TIME

1. Felled by Hiram Wallace during storm
2. Wheeze's crabbing boat
3. Bag used to put cats in
4. Only island transportation
5. Household remedy made from opium
6. Narrow channel of water
7. They work on the water.
8. Blue crab bursting out of its shell
9. Source of Wheeze's jokes
10. Fork-like device used to retrieve oysters
11. Debuts Caroline as Musetta: La ___
12. Smiled like a man who would sing to the oysters
13. Naval base in Hawaii bombed by Japanese: ___ Harbor
14. Author
15. Baltimore newspaper Wheeze reads
16. Delivers babies

A=8	B=1	C=13	D=12
E=11	F=14	G=2	H=7
I=10	J=15	K=3	L=6
M=5	N=4	O=16	P=9

Jacob Have I Loved Magic Squares 3

Match the definition with the vocabulary word. Put your answers in the magic squares below. When your answers are correct, all columns and rows will add to the same number.

A. PEABODY
B. PARIS
C. SUSAN
D. METHODISM
E. CULLING
F. LADIES
G. FDR
H. RICE
I. GUNNYSACK
J. ESAU
K. PIANO
L. HITLER
M. SKIPJACK
N. BOOMERANG
O. DREDGES
P. JOSEPH

1. He has a fiance in Baltimore.
2. Baltimore music school
3. Place Susan wanted to go to write poetry
4. 32nd President of the U.S.
5. Swindled out of birthright by Biblical twin
6. Large frames with nets used to collect shellfish
7. Smiled like a man who would sing to the oysters
8. Bag used to put cats in
9. Instrument owned only by Bradshaws on island
10. Came back every time the Australian threw it
11. Waterman's vessel
12. Dictator of German Nazi party
13. Sorting shellfish by size
14. Island religion
15. Came to Rass to teach
16. Women's group from church: ___ Society

A=	B=	C=	D=
E=	F=	G=	H=
I=	J=	K=	L=
M=	N=	O=	P=

Jacob Have I Loved Magic Squares 3 Answer Key

Match the definition with the vocabulary word. Put your answers in the magic squares below. When your answers are correct, all columns and rows will add to the same number.

A. PEABODY
B. PARIS
C. SUSAN
D. METHODISM
E. CULLING
F. LADIES
G. FDR
H. RICE
I. GUNNYSACK
J. ESAU
K. PIANO
L. HITLER
M. SKIPJACK
N. BOOMERANG
O. DREDGES
P. JOSEPH

1. He has a fiance in Baltimore.
2. Baltimore music school
3. Place Susan wanted to go to write poetry
4. 32nd President of the U.S.
5. Swindled out of birthright by Biblical twin
6. Large frames with nets used to collect shellfish
7. Smiled like a man who would sing to the oysters
8. Bag used to put cats in
9. Instrument owned only by Bradshaws on island
10. Came back every time the Australian threw it
11. Waterman's vessel
12. Dictator of German Nazi party
13. Sorting shellfish by size
14. Island religion
15. Came to Rass to teach
16. Women's group from church: ___ Society

A=2	B=3	C=15	D=14
E=13	F=16	G=4	H=1
I=8	J=5	K=9	L=12
M=11	N=10	O=6	P=7

Jacob Have I Loved Magic Squares 4

Match the definition with the vocabulary word. Put your answers in the magic squares below. When your answers are correct, all columns and rows will add to the same number.

A. CRISFIELD
B. COUNTERSPY
C. JEAN
D. BRADSHAW
E. RICE
F. LADIES
G. BOHEME
H. METHODISM
I. PROG
J. BLACKOUT
K. PEABODY
L. SEARS
M. SKIFF
N. ESAU
O. HURRICANE
P. KENTUCKY

1. Maryland town closest to Rass by ferry
2. Swindled out of birthright by Biblical twin
3. Darkened window coverings: ___ curtains
4. He has a fiance in Baltimore.
5. Debuts Caroline as Musetta: La ___
6. Store where islanders order shoes
7. Graduated a nurse-midwife from Rass
8. Betty ___ sings at the Christmas program.
9. It reduced island cat population by two-thirds.
10. Waterman father of twins: Mr. ___
11. Island religion
12. Baltimore music school
13. To fish for crab
14. Women's group from church: ___ Society
15. Spies on another spy
16. Wheeze's crabbing boat

A=	B=	C=	D=
E=	F=	G=	H=
I=	J=	K=	L=
M=	N=	O=	P=

Jacob Have I Loved Magic Squares 4 Answer Key

Match the definition with the vocabulary word. Put your answers in the magic squares below. When your answers are correct, all columns and rows will add to the same number.

- A. CRISFIELD
- B. COUNTERSPY
- C. JEAN
- D. BRADSHAW
- E. RICE
- F. LADIES
- G. BOHEME
- H. METHODISM
- I. PROG
- J. BLACKOUT
- K. PEABODY
- L. SEARS
- M. SKIFF
- N. ESAU
- O. HURRICANE
- P. KENTUCKY

1. Maryland town closest to Rass by ferry
2. Swindled out of birthright by Biblical twin
3. Darkened window coverings: ___ curtains
4. He has a fiance in Baltimore.
5. Debuts Caroline as Musetta: La ___
6. Store where islanders order shoes
7. Graduated a nurse-midwife from Rass
8. Betty ___ sings at the Christmas program.
9. It reduced island cat population by two-thirds.
10. Waterman father of twins: Mr. ___
11. Island religion
12. Baltimore music school
13. To fish for crab
14. Women's group from church: ___ Society
15. Spies on another spy
16. Wheeze's crabbing boat

A=1	B=15	C=8	D=10
E=4	F=14	G=5	H=11
I=13	J=3	K=12	L=6
M=16	N=2	O=9	P=7

Jacob Have I Loved Word Search 1

```
C O U N T E R S P Y D W F E R R Y X
B C J A R Z D A E S R O K S A E S Y
L D E S U E F B P E N G A N T M B
A E R U D E L B R A D H U K S D X
C C G S Y H C A R G E U J F U N M
K I E A P W U T D E E R W Q B A W
O F N O C Y L H T G S T R D D R L Y
U I S Y G Y L C K O S S I A Y A N G
T C T S Y U I E R R K H C L S D I C
C A P T A I N U S I P I A N O S A B
X P S E S T G N P C S N N D Z H M S
J A M R U X M J Y V D F E D O A N Z
M I A C G K A R C S S K I F F W I M
T E K O O C K I A C A P J E A N G S
S Y R O K N X C L S Q C C N L U H Y
B P S C J Z R E L T I H K A T D T Z
```

32nd President of the U.S. (3)
Bag used to put cats in (9)
Baltimore newspaper Wheeze reads (3)
Betty ___ sings at the Christmas program. (4)
Blue crab bursting out of its shell (6)
Blue crab ready to shed its shell: ___ peeler (4)
Came to Rass to teach (5)
Caroline's Christmas solo: I ___ As I ___ (6)
Chesapeake island near Crisfield (4)
Continental part of state (8)
Darkened window coverings: ___ curtains (8)
Dictator of German Nazi party (6)
Earned title of fifty year old waterman (7)
Felled by Hiram Wallace during storm (4)
Fuel for scriptural quote by Grandma (6)
Gets thrown against a wall (7)
Graduated a nurse-midwife from Rass (8)
He has a fiance in Baltimore. (4)
Holy day (7)
Household remedy made from opium (9)
Instrument owned only by Bradshaws on island (5)
It reduced island cat population by two-thirds. (9)
Knows what evil lurks in the hearts of men: The ___ (6)
Lady crab (4)

Large frames with nets used to collect shellfish (7)
Maryland town closest to Rass by ferry (9)
Mc___ Purnell (4)
Narrow channel of water (3)
Naval base in Hawaii bombed by Japanese: ___ Harbor (5)
Only island transportation (5)
Sara Louise's nickname (6)
Shells on island streets (6)
Sorting shellfish by size (7)
Source of Wheeze's jokes (4)
Spies on another spy (10)
Store where islanders order shoes (5)
Sung by Betty Jean Boyd: O Holy ___ (5)
Swindled out of birthright by Biblical twin (4)
Three island boys aboard the same ship died there: South ___ (7)
To fish for crab (4)
University Wheeze first attends (8)
Waterman father of twins: Mr. ___ (8)
Waterman's vessel (8)
Wheeze's crabbing boat (5)
Where Wheeze wants to take the cats (4)
Woman Hiram marries (5)

Jacob Have I Loved Word Search 1 Answer Key

```
C  O  U  N  T  E  R  S  P  Y     D  W  F  E  R  R  Y
B     J  A  R  Z  D  A  E        R  O     S  A  E
L     E  S  U  E  F  B  P        E  N     A  N  T
A  E  R  U  D  E     B  R        D  D  H  U  K  S  D
C  C  G  S  Y  H  C  A  L        G  E  U        U     M
K  I  E  A     W  U  T           E  R  R        B  N  A
O  F  N  O  C     L  H           S     R        R     L
U  I  S  Y  G  Y  L  C  K  O     S  S  I  A  Y  A     N
T  C  S     U  I  E  R  R  S  I  K  H  C  L  S  D     I
C     P  T  A  I  N  U  S  P  C  P  I  A  N  O  S     A
   P  S  E  S  T  G  N  P  Y     S  N  N  D     H     M
   A  M  R  U        J     C     D  F  E        O     N
M  I  A  C  G  K  A  R  C  S     S  K  I  F  F  W     I
T  E  K  O  O  C     I  A        A  P  J  E  A  N     G
S  Y  R  O  K        C  L        C  C     L  U  H
P  S              R  E  L  T  I  H  K  A  T  D  T
```

32nd President of the U.S. (3)
Bag used to put cats in (9)
Baltimore newspaper Wheeze reads (3)
Betty ___ sings at the Christmas program. (4)
Blue crab bursting out of its shell (6)
Blue crab ready to shed its shell: ___ peeler (4)
Came to Rass to teach (5)
Caroline's Christmas solo: I ___ As I ___ (6)
Chesapeake island near Crisfield (4)
Continental part of state (8)
Darkened window coverings: ___ curtains (8)
Dictator of German Nazi party (6)
Earned title of fifty year old waterman (7)
Felled by Hiram Wallace during storm (4)
Fuel for scriptural quote by Grandma (6)
Gets thrown against a wall (7)
Graduated a nurse-midwife from Rass (8)
He has a fiance in Baltimore. (4)
Holy day (7)
Household remedy made from opium (9)
Instrument owned only by Bradshaws on island (5)
It reduced island cat population by two-thirds. (9)
Knows what evil lurks in the hearts of men: The ___ (6)
Lady crab (4)

Large frames with nets used to collect shellfish (7)
Maryland town closest to Rass by ferry (9)
Mc____ Purnell (4)
Narrow channel of water (3)
Naval base in Hawaii bombed by Japanese: ___ Harbor (5)
Only island transportation (5)
Sara Louise's nickname (6)
Shells on island streets (6)
Sorting shellfish by size (7)
Source of Wheeze's jokes (4)
Spies on another spy (10)
Store where islanders order shoes (5)
Sung by Betty Jean Boyd: O Holy ___ (5)
Swindled out of birthright by Biblical twin (4)
Three island boys aboard the same ship died there: South ___ (7)
To fish for crab (4)
University Wheeze first attends (8)
Waterman father of twins: Mr. ___ (8)
Waterman's vessel (8)
Wheeze's crabbing boat (5)
Where Wheeze wants to take the cats (4)
Woman Hiram marries (5)

Jacob Have I Loved Word Search 2

```
S D L E G A C Y U S X P V P Y S J Y
K L J W W P L Q N O K O L I R P E V
I E J O S E P H L O P K M A U C A W
F I S I R A P N I K W E W N B A N O
F F V E G B W D M R R A O S Z K D
T S C D F O L A I E A Y O R I E D A
J I M M Y D U R T S A M R E L T I H
R R M V P Y R S E E E B S L A C T S
X C G E S Y Y K D R R W A B S A S W
S Y X L R O R E A V S M P H B A N N
E J F R E T O N G S S H E B R I G
A S E F T P G T N L J C A N Y A G V
R F A L N R V U M S U S A N T N H K
S C L U U O V C I F I C A P T K T T
X A Y C O G V K G U T Y A N H Y L Q
C S U N C D D Y B L A C K O U T C S
```

32nd President of the U.S. (3)
Baltimore music school (7)
Baltimore newspaper Wheeze reads (3)
Betty ___ sings at the Christmas program. (4)
Blue crab ready to shed its shell: ___ peeler (4)
Came back every time the Australian threw it (9)
Came to Rass to teach (5)
Chesapeake island near Crisfield (4)
Crab shack (6)
Darkened window coverings: ___ curtains (8)
Dictator of German Nazi party (6)
Earned title of fifty year old waterman (7)
Felled by Hiram Wallace during storm (4)
Fork-like device used to retrieve oysters (5)
Fuel for scriptural quote by Grandma (6)
General store and post office on island (7)
Graduated a nurse-midwife from Rass (8)
He has a fiance in Baltimore. (4)
Holy day (7)
Inland Eastern Shore Maryland town (9)
Instrument owned only by Bradshaws on island (5)
Island native who returns after 50 years (5)
Knows what evil lurks in the hearts of men: The ___ (6)
Lady crab (4)

Lyrics ___ misspelled Wheeze's name on form letter (9)
Male blue crab (5)
Maryland town closest to Rass by ferry (9)
Mc___ Purnell (4)
Narrow channel of water (3)
Naval base in Hawaii bombed by Japanese: ___ Harbor (5)
Only island transportation (5)
Place Susan wanted to go to write poetry (5)
Shells on island streets (6)
Smiled like a man who would sing to the oysters (6)
Source of Wheeze's jokes (4)
Spies on another spy (10)
Store where islanders order shoes (5)
Sung by Betty Jean Boyd: O Holy ___ (5)
Swindled out of birthright by Biblical twin (4)
They work on the water. (8)
Three island boys aboard the same ship died there: South ___ (7)
To fish for crab (4)
Wheeze beats Caroline satisfactorily at it (5)
Wheeze's crabbing boat (5)
Where Wheeze wants to take the cats (4)
Woman Hiram marries (5)

Jacob Have I Loved Word Search 2 Answer Key

```
S   D   L   E   G   A   C   Y   U   S       P       P   Y   S   J
K   L           P           N   O       P   O       I   R   P   E
I   E   J   O   S   E   P   H   L   O   P   K       A   U   C   A   W
F   I   S   I   R   A   P       I   K       E       N   B   A   N   O
F   F       E       B   W       M   R   R   A   O   S       K       D
T   S   C       F   O       A   I   E   A       O   R   I   E       A
J   I   M   M   Y   D   U   R   T   S   A   M   R   E   L   T   I   H
R   R   M       P   Y   R   S   E   E   E       L   A       T   S
    C       E   S   Y   Y   K   D   R   R       A   S   A   S
S           R   O       E   A       S   M       B   A   N       N
E           R   E   T   O   N   G   S   S   H   E   B   R   R   I
A   S   E       T   P   G   T           A   N       A       G
R   F   A   L   N   R       U       S   U   S   A   N   T   N   H
S       L   U   U   O   C   I   F   I   C   A   P   T   K   T
        A       O   G   K   G   U   T       A       Y
C   S   U   N   C       Y   B   L   A   C   K   O   U   T
```

32nd President of the U.S. (3)
Baltimore music school (7)
Baltimore newspaper Wheeze reads (3)
Betty ___ sings at the Christmas program. (4)
Blue crab ready to shed its shell: ___ peeler (4)
Came back every time the Australian threw it (9)
Came to Rass to teach (5)
Chesapeake island near Crisfield (4)
Crab shack (6)
Darkened window coverings: ___ curtains (8)
Dictator of German Nazi party (6)
Earned title of fifty year old waterman (7)
Felled by Hiram Wallace during storm (4)
Fork-like device used to retrieve oysters (5)
Fuel for scriptural quote by Grandma (6)
General store and post office on island (7)
Graduated a nurse-midwife from Rass (8)
He has a fiance in Baltimore. (4)
Holy day (7)
Inland Eastern Shore Maryland town (9)
Instrument owned only by Bradshaws on island (5)
Island native who returns after 50 years (5)
Knows what evil lurks in the hearts of men: The ___ (6)
Lady crab (4)

Lyrics ___ misspelled Wheeze's name on form letter (9)
Male blue crab (5)
Maryland town closest to Rass by ferry (9)
Mc____ Purnell (4)
Narrow channel of water (3)
Naval base in Hawaii bombed by Japanese: ___ Harbor (5)
Only island transportation (5)
Place Susan wanted to go to write poetry (5)
Shells on island streets (6)
Smiled like a man who would sing to the oysters (6)
Source of Wheeze's jokes (4)
Spies on another spy (10)
Store where islanders order shoes (5)
Sung by Betty Jean Boyd: O Holy ___ (5)
Swindled out of birthright by Biblical twin (4)
They work on the water. (8)
Three island boys aboard the same ship died there: South ___ (7)
To fish for crab (4)
Wheeze beats Caroline satisfactorily at it (5)
Wheeze's crabbing boat (5)
Where Wheeze wants to take the cats (4)
Woman Hiram marries (5)

Jacob Have I Loved Word Search 3

```
J C A P T A I N E M R E T A W Z S U N P
S O V A Z Q W C L W F S K K R E D N O W
F D S T Y D O B A E P A E M R P K K S L
C R B E H W D P W R R U L E K L E P X P
B E U R P F A S E I D A P A R I S J Y T
L D S S T H H T Y R H T A J S A S B Y K
A G T O H D S K S B I N M F N W K O R F
C E E N X Y R Y P H H S O F H I O U Z
K S R E O J R N E Q T J C N R E P M B Q
O M M B J R S R A N A A T O D E J E S C
U I K J E E W R L B C X L P Z A R I D
T C I F I C A P L F B O H E M E C A L L
H R M M M H R N F A A B F S S A K N A B
G H U W S P S I L B S I I Z X S G S X
I M R D M X K T B S W D U S H A N T Y D
N W A R Y S I H G D O O F U R G E R Z N
C R T T R M G N I H L O K S A B G U A R
B U N T O O O M T R Y N K A S B R I C E
G K Z R R T H E W S A Z Y N S D E T P H
N V E P J I M M Y R C M D F F J J T S X
```

BALTIMORE	GUT	METHODISM	PROG	SPCA
BLACKOUT	HIRAM	MIDWIFE	RANK	SUN
BOHEME	HITLER	NIGHT	RASS	SUSAN
BOOMERANG	JACOB	OYSTER	RICE	TIME
BRADSHAW	JEAN	PACIFIC	SABBATH	TONGS
BUSTER	JERGENS	PARIS	SALISBURY	TRUDY
CALL	JIMMY	PATERSON	SEARS	TRUITT
CAPTAIN	JOSEPH	PEABODY	SHADOW	WATERMEN
DREDGES	KELLAMS	PEARL	SHANTY	WHEEZE
ESAU	LADIES	PERISCOPE	SKIFF	WONDER
FDR	LOUISE	PIANO	SKIPJACK	
FERRY	MAST	POKER	SOOK	

Jacob Have I Loved Word Search 3 Answer Key

BALTIMORE	GUT	METHODISM	PROG	SPCA
BLACKOUT	HIRAM	MIDWIFE	RANK	SUN
BOHEME	HITLER	NIGHT	RASS	SUSAN
BOOMERANG	JACOB	OYSTER	RICE	TIME
BRADSHAW	JEAN	PACIFIC	SABBATH	TONGS
BUSTER	JERGENS	PARIS	SALISBURY	TRUDY
CALL	JIMMY	PATERSON	SEARS	TRUITT
CAPTAIN	JOSEPH	PEABODY	SHADOW	WATERMEN
DREDGES	KELLAMS	PEARL	SHANTY	WHEEZE
ESAU	LADIES	PERISCOPE	SKIFF	WONDER
FDR	LOUISE	PIANO	SKIPJACK	
FERRY	MAST	POKER	SOOK	

Jacob Have I Loved Word Search 4

```
P G Z N P O K E R H P G J K L P I A N O
A Y V E A C T F V H O H V O A F J S Y K
T V D M R I R I J R J H U L D M L F C M
E Y R R E F U W P E M I T N I A T P A G
R B A E G I I D E M S R M L E R O I G G
S O I T O C T I A E Z A J M S Y N Q E D
O O L A R A T M B H M M B E Y L G L L Z
N M L W I P M S O O B O K R A A S V K G
D E I L C T E A D B C N U N F N X J C L
R R U E D R T B Y A S F D N R D B E A L
E A J E S U H B J Y H B U S T E R J X
D N V L X D O A V W A S G R G A G P R
G G M G O Y D T A J N P S L U G I E I F
E M M R N Y I H F Q T C F U N Z M N K E
S J S A L I S B U R Y A K I N R A S S T
T P S S S D M T Z Z F N L I Y W J A K Q
Z U A S A T K R E R A L G G S C U Z I X
S S L R A E P J I R U H F U A O A K F R
Q M B H I T L E R C T Z D T C Q O L F L
D L E I F S I R C S E A R S K L F K L J
```

BOHEME	FERRY	LOUISE	PATERSON	SHANTY
BOOMERANG	GUNNYSACK	MAINLAND	PEABODY	SKIFF
BRADSHAW	GUT	MARYLAND	PEARL	SKIPJACK
BUSTER	HIRAM	MAST	PIANO	SOOK
CALL	HITLER	METHODISM	POKER	SPCA
CAPTAIN	JACOB	MIDWIFE	PROG	SUN
CRISFIELD	JEAN	MOUNTAINS	RANK	SUSAN
CULLING	JERGENS	NIGHT	RASS	TIME
DREDGES	JIMMY	OYSTER	RICE	TONGS
EELGRASS	JUILLIARD	PACIFIC	SABBATH	TRUDY
ESAU	LADIES	PAREGORIC	SALISBURY	TRUITT
FDR	LEGACY	PARIS	SEARS	WATERMEN

Jacob Have I Loved Word Search 4 Answer Key

BOHEME	FERRY	LOUISE	PATERSON	SHANTY
BOOMERANG	GUNNYSACK	MAINLAND	PEABODY	SKIFF
BRADSHAW	GUT	MARYLAND	PEARL	SKIPJACK
BUSTER	HIRAM	MAST	PIANO	SOOK
CALL	HITLER	METHODISM	POKER	SPCA
CAPTAIN	JACOB	MIDWIFE	PROG	SUN
CRISFIELD	JEAN	MOUNTAINS	RANK	SUSAN
CULLING	JERGENS	NIGHT	RASS	TIME
DREDGES	JIMMY	OYSTER	RICE	TONGS
EELGRASS	JUILLIARD	PACIFIC	SABBATH	TRUDY
ESAU	LADIES	PAREGORIC	SALISBURY	TRUITT
FDR	LEGACY	PARIS	SEARS	WATERMEN

Jacob Have I Loved Crossword 1

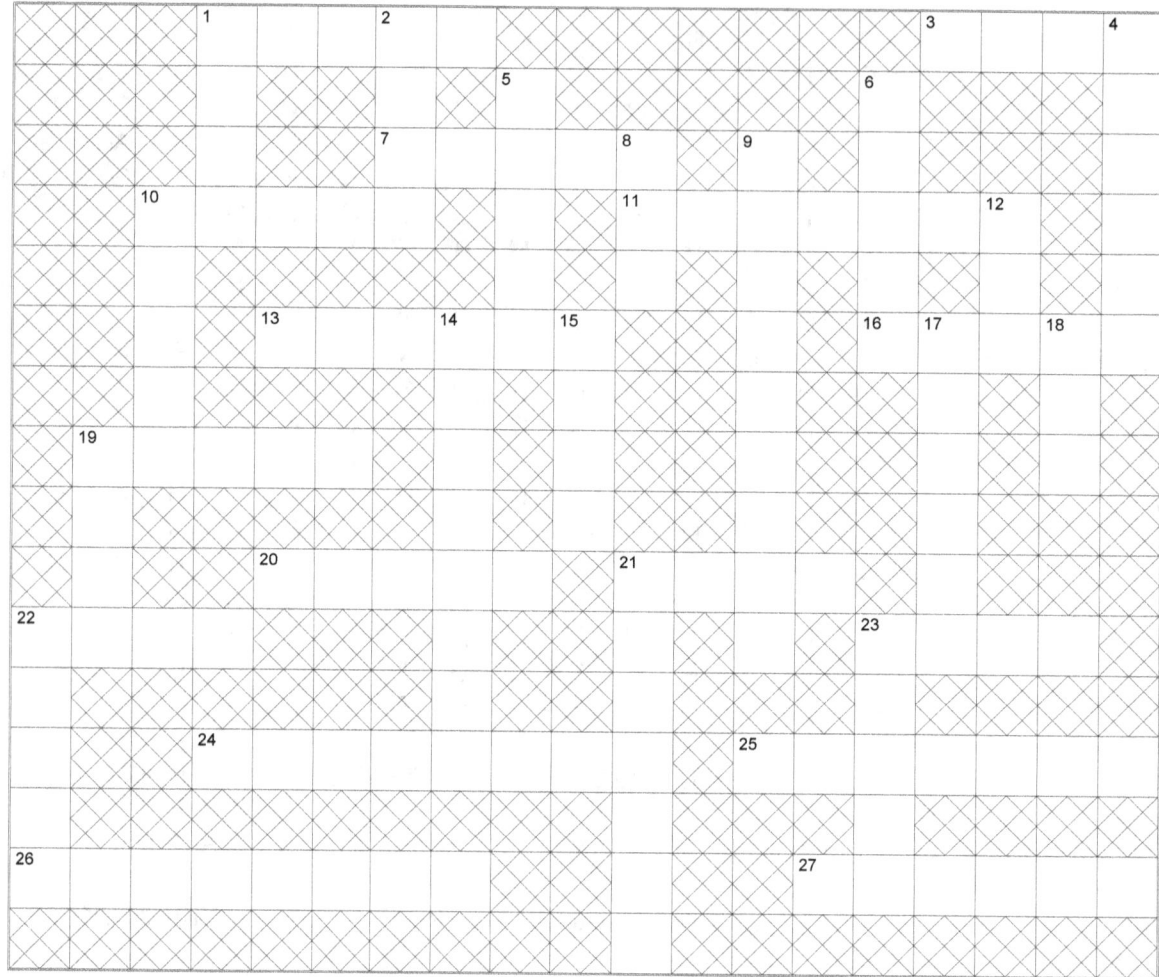

Across
1. Store where islanders order shoes
3. Mc____ Purnell
7. Wheeze's crabbing boat
10. Place Susan wanted to go to write poetry
11. Large frames with nets used to collect shellfish
13. Debuts Caroline as Musetta: La ___
16. Fork-like device used to retrieve oysters
19. Woman Hiram marries
20. Only island transportation
21. Felled by Hiram Wallace during storm
22. Betty ___ sings at the Christmas program.
23. To fish for crab
24. Waterman father of twins: Mr. ___
25. Baltimore music school
26. Darkened window coverings: ___ curtains
27. Caroline's Christmas solo: I ___ As I ___

Down
1. Where Wheeze wants to take the cats
2. Chesapeake island near Crisfield
4. Women's group from church: ___ Society
5. Island native who returns after 50 years
6. Sung by Betty Jean Boyd: O Holy ___
8. 32nd President of the U.S.
9. Island religion
10. Wheeze beats Caroline satisfactorily at it
12. Baltimore newspaper Wheeze reads
14. Marine plant with ribbon-like leaves
15. Swindled out of birthright by Biblical twin
17. Shells on island streets
18. Narrow channel of water
19. Source of Wheeze's jokes
21. Delivers babies
22. Tricks blind father in Bible out of birthright
23. Instrument owned only by Bradshaws on island

Jacob Have I Loved Crossword 1 Answer Key

			1 S	E	A	2 R	S				3 C	A	L	4 L
			P			A		5 H		6 N				A
			C			7 S	K	I	8 F	9 M	I			D
		10 P	A	R	I	S		R	11 D	R	E	D	12 G	E	S	I
		O						A	R				H		U		E
		K		13 B	O	14 H	E	15 M	E			16 T	17 O	N	18 G	S
		E				E		S				Y			U	
	19 T	R	U	D	Y		L		A			D			S		T
	I					G		U				I			T	
	M			20 F	E	R	R	Y		21 M	A	S	T		E
22 J	E	A	N			A				I			M		23 P	R	O	G
A						S				D					I
C				24 B	R	A	D	S	H	A	W		25 P	E	A	B	O	D	Y
O										W					N
26 B	L	A	C	K	O	U	T		I	F		27 W	O	N	D	E	R
										E

Across
1. Store where islanders order shoes
3. Mc____ Purnell
7. Wheeze's crabbing boat
10. Place Susan wanted to go to write poetry
11. Large frames with nets used to collect shellfish
13. Debuts Caroline as Musetta: La ___
16. Fork-like device used to retrieve oysters
19. Woman Hiram marries
20. Only island transportation
21. Felled by Hiram Wallace during storm
22. Betty ___ sings at the Christmas program.
23. To fish for crab
24. Waterman father of twins: Mr. ___
25. Baltimore music school
26. Darkened window coverings: ___ curtains
27. Caroline's Christmas solo: I ___ As I ___

Down
1. Where Wheeze wants to take the cats
2. Chesapeake island near Crisfield
4. Women's group from church: ___ Society
5. Island native who returns after 50 years
6. Sung by Betty Jean Boyd: O Holy ___
8. 32nd President of the U.S.
9. Island religion
10. Wheeze beats Caroline satisfactorily at it
12. Baltimore newspaper Wheeze reads
14. Marine plant with ribbon-like leaves
15. Swindled out of birthright by Biblical twin
17. Shells on island streets
18. Narrow channel of water
19. Source of Wheeze's jokes
21. Delivers babies
22. Tricks blind father in Bible out of birthright
23. Instrument owned only by Bradshaws on island

Jacob Have I Loved Crossword 2

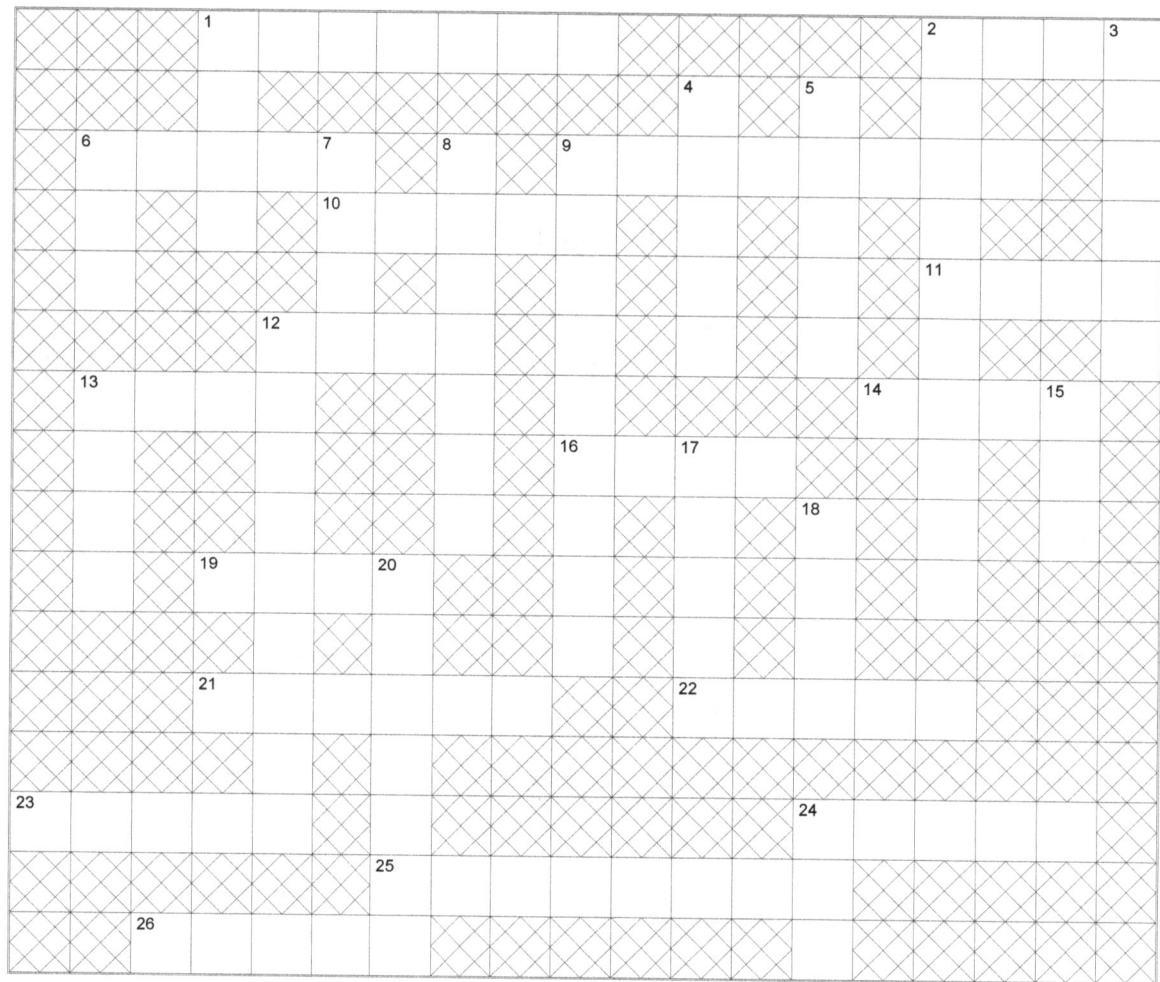

Across
1. Gets thrown against a wall
2. Mc____ Purnell
6. Store where islanders order shoes
9. Darkened window coverings: ___ curtains
10. Instrument owned only by Bradshaws on island
11. Source of Wheeze's jokes
12. Felled by Hiram Wallace during storm
13. He has a fiance in Baltimore.
14. To fish for crab
16. Blue crab ready to shed its shell: ___ peeler
19. Lady crab
21. Dictator of German Nazi party
22. Woman Hiram marries
23. Island native who returns after 50 years
24. Only island transportation
25. Continental part of state
26. Fork-like device used to retrieve oysters

Down
1. Betty ___ sings at the Christmas program.
2. Spies on another spy
3. Women's group from church: ___ Society
4. Place Susan wanted to go to write poetry
5. Wheeze's crabbing boat
6. Baltimore newspaper Wheeze reads
7. Where Wheeze wants to take the cats
8. Earned title of fifty year old waterman
9. Came back every time the Australian threw it
12. Island religion
13. Chesapeake island near Crisfield
15. Narrow channel of water
17. Sung by Betty Jean Boyd: O Holy ___
18. Swindled out of birthright by Biblical twin
20. General store and post office on island
24. 32nd President of the U.S.

Jacob Have I Loved Crossword 2 Answer Key

			1 J	E	R	G	E	N	S				2 C	A	L	3 L
			E							4 P	5 S		O			A
	6 S	E	A	R	7 S		8 C		9 B	L	A	C	K	O	U	T	D
	U		N		10 P	I	A	N	O		R		I		N		I
	N				C		P		O		I		F		11 T	I	M	E
			12 M	A	S	T		M		S		F		E			S
13 R	I	C	E					E				14 P	R	O	15 G	
	A		T				16 R	A	17 N	K			S		U	
	S		H				I		E			18 P		T	
	S		19 S	O	20 O	K		N		G		S		Y	
					D		E				G		H		A	
			21 H	I	T	L	E	R			22 T	R	U	D	Y	
					S		L								
23 H	I	R	A	M		A						24 F	E	R	R	Y
				25 M	A	I	N	L	A	N	D			
			26 T	O	N	G	S				R		

Across
1. Gets thrown against a wall
2. Mc____ Purnell
6. Store where islanders order shoes
9. Darkened window coverings: ___ curtains
10. Instrument owned only by Bradshaws on island
11. Source of Wheeze's jokes
12. Felled by Hiram Wallace during storm
13. He has a fiance in Baltimore.
14. To fish for crab
16. Blue crab ready to shed its shell: ___ peeler
19. Lady crab
21. Dictator of German Nazi party
22. Woman Hiram marries
23. Island native who returns after 50 years
24. Only island transportation
25. Continental part of state
26. Fork-like device used to retrieve oysters

Down
1. Betty ___ sings at the Christmas program.
2. Spies on another spy
3. Women's group from church: ___ Society
4. Place Susan wanted to go to write poetry
5. Wheeze's crabbing boat
6. Baltimore newspaper Wheeze reads
7. Where Wheeze wants to take the cats
8. Earned title of fifty year old waterman
9. Came back every time the Australian threw it
12. Island religion
13. Chesapeake island near Crisfield
15. Narrow channel of water
17. Sung by Betty Jean Boyd: O Holy ___
18. Swindled out of birthright by Biblical twin
20. General store and post office on island
24. 32nd President of the U.S.

Jacob Have I Loved Crossword 3

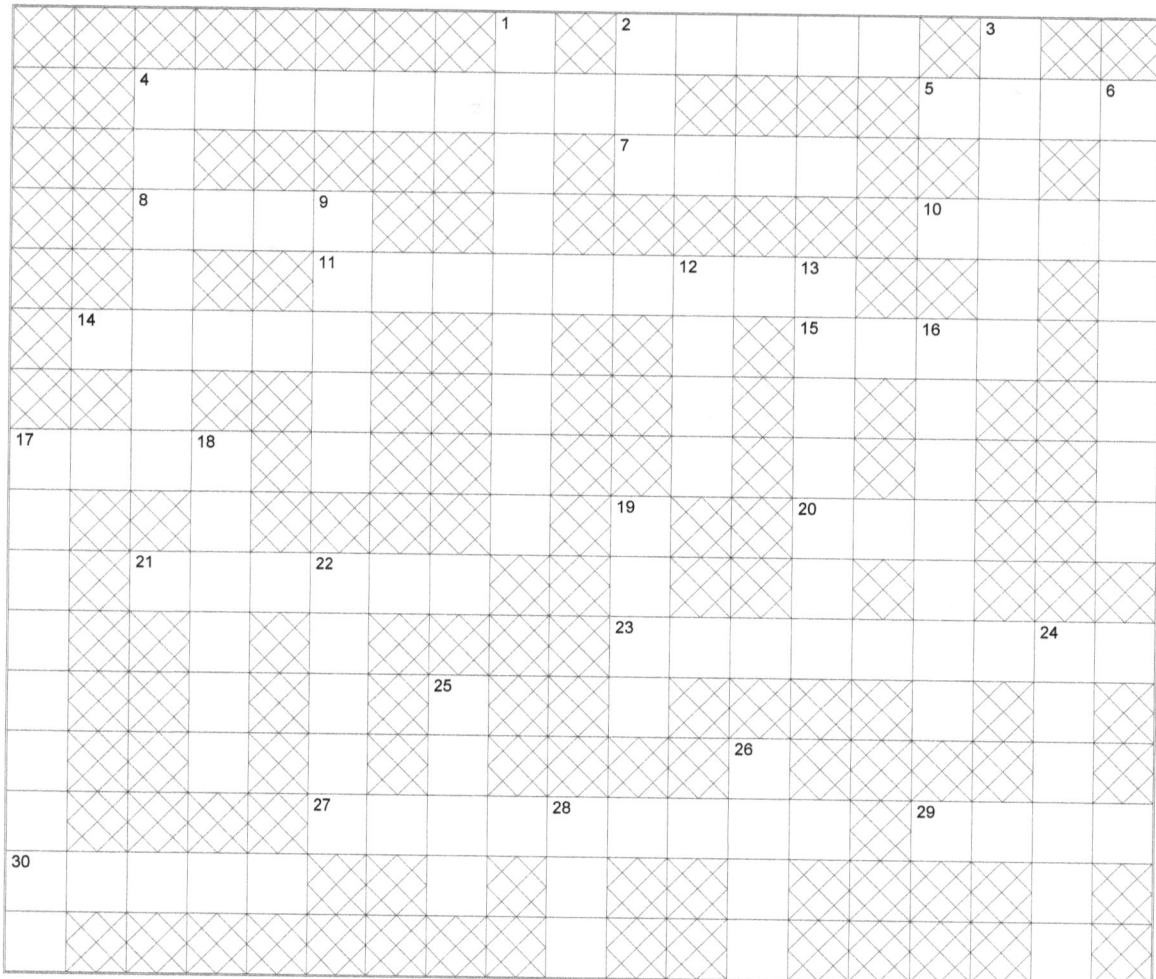

Across
2. Only island transportation
4. New York City music conservatory
5. Lady crab
7. Blue crab ready to shed its shell: ___ peeler
8. Chesapeake island near Crisfield
10. Betty ___ sings at the Christmas program.
11. Lyrics ___ misspelled Wheeze's name on form letter
14. Store where islanders order shoes
15. He has a fiance in Baltimore.
17. Felled by Hiram Wallace during storm
20. Narrow channel of water
21. Blue crab bursting out of its shell
23. Maryland town closest to Rass by ferry
27. Inland Eastern Shore Maryland town
29. Swindled out of birthright by Biblical twin
30. Sung by Betty Jean Boyd: O Holy ___

Down
1. Large Maryland seaport
2. 32nd President of the U.S.
3. Debuts Caroline as Musetta: La ___
4. Gets thrown against a wall
6. Graduated a nurse-midwife from Rass
9. Came to Rass to teach
12. Source of Wheeze's jokes
13. Large frames with nets used to collect shellfish
16. Earned title of fifty year old waterman
17. Wheeze longs to see them.
18. Mountain-locked Appalachian valley
19. Where Wheeze wants to take the cats
22. Fork-like device used to retrieve oysters
24. Fuel for scriptural quote by Grandma
25. Mc____ Purnell
26. To fish for crab
28. Baltimore newspaper Wheeze reads

Jacob Have I Loved Crossword 3 Answer Key

						¹B		²F	E	R	R	Y		³B	
		⁴J	U	I	L	L	I	A	R	D			⁵S	O	O	⁶K
		E				L		⁷R	A	N	K			H		E
	⁸R	A	S	⁹S		T							¹⁰J	E	A	N
		G		¹¹U	N	L	I	M	I	¹²T	¹³E	D			M		T
	¹⁴S	E	A	R	S			M		I		R	I	¹⁶C	E		U
		N			A			O		M		E		A			C
¹⁷M	A	¹⁸S		N			R			E		D		²⁰G	U	T		K
O		R				E		¹⁹S		G	U	T		A			Y
U	²¹B	U	S	²²T	E	R		P		E		A			
N		I		O				²³C	R	I	S	F	I	E	²⁴L	D
T		T		N		²⁵C		A				N		E	
A		T		G		A				²⁶P				G	
I			²⁷S	A	L	I	²⁸S	B	U	R	Y		²⁹E	S	A	U
³⁰N	I	G	H	T		L		U		O				C	
S								N		G				Y	

Across
2. Only island transportation
4. New York City music conservatory
5. Lady crab
7. Blue crab ready to shed its shell: ___ peeler
8. Chesapeake island near Crisfield
10. Betty ___ sings at the Christmas program.
11. Lyrics ___ misspelled Wheeze's name on form letter
14. Store where islanders order shoes
15. He has a fiance in Baltimore.
17. Felled by Hiram Wallace during storm
20. Narrow channel of water
21. Blue crab bursting out of its shell
23. Maryland town closest to Rass by ferry
27. Inland Eastern Shore Maryland town
29. Swindled out of birthright by Biblical twin
30. Sung by Betty Jean Boyd: O Holy ___

Down
1. Large Maryland seaport
2. 32nd President of the U.S.
3. Debuts Caroline as Musetta: La ___
4. Gets thrown against a wall
6. Graduated a nurse-midwife from Rass
9. Came to Rass to teach
12. Source of Wheeze's jokes
13. Large frames with nets used to collect shellfish
16. Earned title of fifty year old waterman
17. Wheeze longs to see them.
18. Mountain-locked Appalachian valley
19. Where Wheeze wants to take the cats
22. Fork-like device used to retrieve oysters
24. Fuel for scriptural quote by Grandma
25. Mc___ Purnell
26. To fish for crab
28. Baltimore newspaper Wheeze reads

Jacob Have I Loved Crossword 4

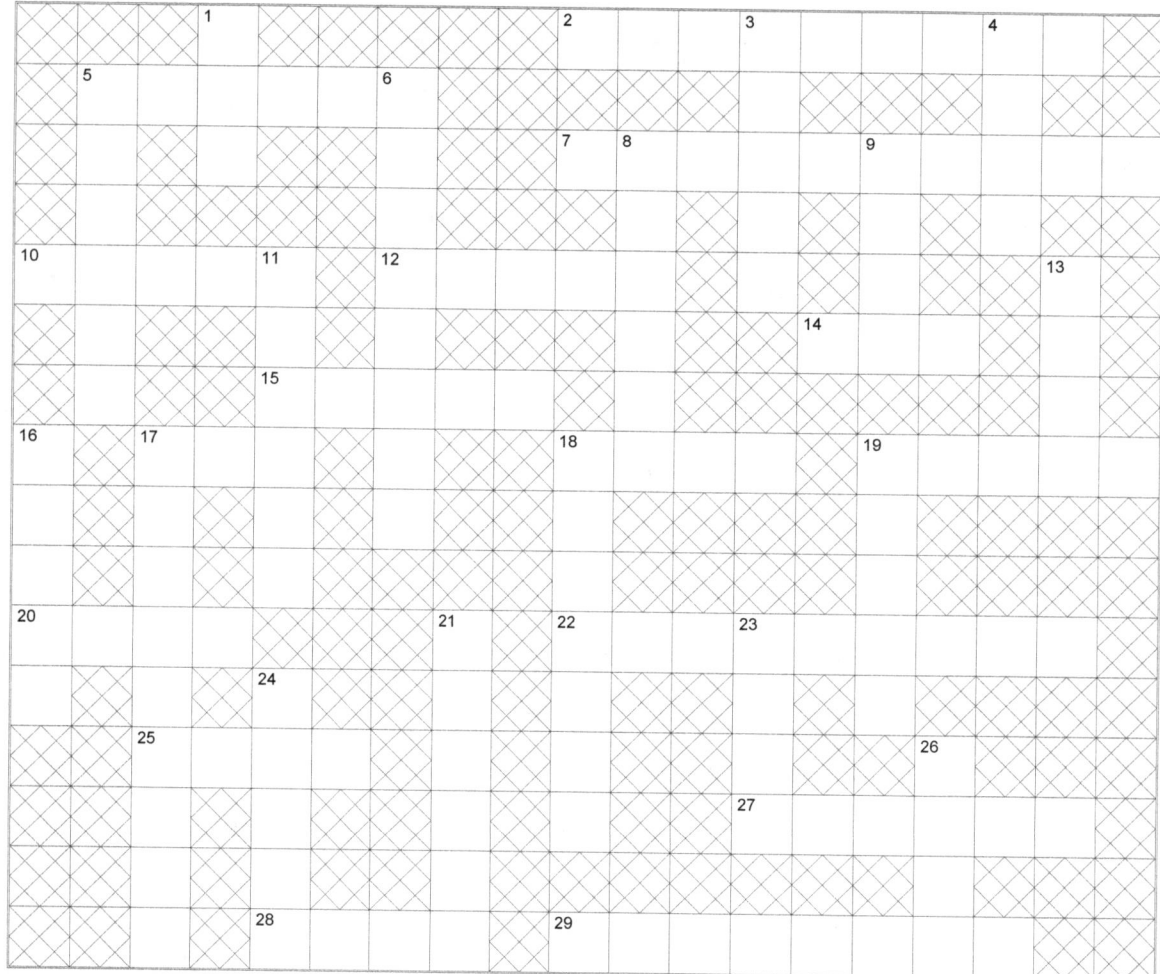

Across
2. Large Maryland seaport
5. Women's group from church: ___ Society
7. Spies on another spy
10. Tricks blind father in Bible out of birthright
12. Place Susan wanted to go to write poetry
14. Baltimore newspaper Wheeze reads
15. Store where islanders order shoes
17. Narrow channel of water
18. To fish for crab
19. Instrument owned only by Bradshaws on island
20. Blue crab ready to shed its shell: ___ peeler
22. Came back every time the Australian threw it
25. Lady crab
27. Mountain-locked Appalachian valley
28. He has a fiance in Baltimore.
29. They work on the water.

Down
1. 32nd President of the U.S.
3. Fork-like device used to retrieve oysters
4. Chesapeake island near Crisfield
5. Fuel for scriptural quote by Grandma
6. Waterman's vessel
8. Shells on island streets
9. Swindled out of birthright by Biblical twin
11. Blue crab bursting out of its shell
13. Betty ___ sings at the Christmas program.
16. Only island transportation
17. Bag used to put cats in
18. Baltimore music school
19. Naval base in Hawaii bombed by Japanese: ___ Harbor
21. Sara Louise's nickname
23. Felled by Hiram Wallace during storm
24. Wheeze beats Caroline satisfactorily at it
26. Source of Wheeze's jokes

Jacob Have I Loved Crossword 4 Answer Key

			1 F				2 B	3 A	L	T	I	M	O	4 R	E	
	5 L	A	D	I	E	6 S				O				A		
	E		R			K		7 C	8 O	U	N	T	9 E	R	S	P Y
	G					I		Y		G			S		S	
10 J	A	C	O 11 B		12 P	A	R	I	S		S		A		13 J	
	C		U		J			T			14 S	U	N		E	
	Y		15 S	E	A	R	S		E				A			
16 F		17 G	U	T		C		18 P	R	O	G		19 P	I	A	N O
E		U		E		K		E					E			
R		N		R				A					A			
20 R	A	N	K			21 W		22 B	O	O	23 M	E	R	A	N	G
Y		Y		24 P		H		O			A		L			
				25 S	O	O	K		E		D		A		26 T	
				A		K		E			Y		27 T	R	U	I T T
				C		E		Z							M	
				28 K		R	I	C	E		29 W	A	T	E	R	M E N

Across
2. Large Maryland seaport
5. Women's group from church: ___ Society
7. Spies on another spy
10. Tricks blind father in Bible out of birthright
12. Place Susan wanted to go to write poetry
14. Baltimore newspaper Wheeze reads
15. Store where islanders order shoes
17. Narrow channel of water
18. To fish for crab
19. Instrument owned only by Bradshaws on island
20. Blue crab ready to shed its shell: ___ peeler
22. Came back every time the Australian threw it
25. Lady crab
27. Mountain-locked Appalachian valley
28. He has a fiance in Baltimore.
29. They work on the water.

Down
1. 32nd President of the U.S.
3. Fork-like device used to retrieve oysters
4. Chesapeake island near Crisfield
5. Fuel for scriptural quote by Grandma
6. Waterman's vessel
8. Shells on island streets
9. Swindled out of birthright by Biblical twin
11. Blue crab bursting out of its shell
13. Betty ___ sings at the Christmas program.
16. Only island transportation
17. Bag used to put cats in
18. Baltimore music school
19. Naval base in Hawaii bombed by Japanese: ___ Harbor
21. Sara Louise's nickname
23. Felled by Hiram Wallace during storm
24. Wheeze beats Caroline satisfactorily at it
26. Source of Wheeze's jokes

Jacob Have I Loved

GUNNYSACK	SPCA	HIRAM	EELGRASS	SKIPJACK
UNLIMITED	PIANO	DREDGES	CAPTAIN	KENTUCKY
HURRICANE	CALL	FREE SPACE	HITLER	RASS
BRADSHAW	BOOMERANG	FERRY	TRUDY	TIME
LEGACY	SALISBURY	WONDER	JOSEPH	ESAU

Jacob Have I Loved

JERGENS	OYSTER	SEARS	TRUITT	POKER
PAREGORIC	PACIFIC	LADIES	LOUISE	MAST
BOHEME	SUN	FREE SPACE	MAINLAND	BALTIMORE
PROG	CULLING	JIMMY	SOOK	METHODISM
SHANTY	MIDWIFE	BUSTER	CRISFIELD	WATERMEN

Jacob Have I Loved

PEARL	RICE	FDR	OYSTER	TRUDY
SABBATH	MIDWIFE	PERISCOPE	WATERMEN	LADIES
POKER	SKIFF	FREE SPACE	BOHEME	PARIS
SEARS	HIRAM	METHODISM	ESAU	JACOB
MAST	CAPTAIN	NIGHT	TRUITT	BRADSHAW

Jacob Have I Loved

HURRICANE	KELLAMS	EELGRASS	CALL	BALTIMORE
SUSAN	LOUISE	KENTUCKY	HITLER	BLACKOUT
CRISFIELD	SUN	FREE SPACE	TIME	PACIFIC
COUNTERSPY	PIANO	UNLIMITED	FERRY	JIMMY
JEAN	GUNNYSACK	PEABODY	MAINLAND	TONGS

Jacob Have I Loved

BUSTER	TIME	RICE	TRUITT	LEGACY
MIDWIFE	RASS	SHADOW	MOUNTAINS	FDR
SOOK	SHANTY	FREE SPACE	WONDER	HITLER
UNLIMITED	SALISBURY	PAREGORIC	CAROLINE	JUILLIARD
WATERMEN	HIRAM	SKIPJACK	PACIFIC	KELLAMS

Jacob Have I Loved

LOUISE	GUT	RANK	POKER	ESAU
JEAN	PROG	TRUDY	SPCA	COUNTERSPY
CRISFIELD	PERISCOPE	FREE SPACE	LADIES	OYSTER
METHODISM	SUN	CULLING	JOSEPH	KENTUCKY
BOHEME	MARYLAND	MAST	FERRY	SEARS

Jacob Have I Loved

SEARS	LEGACY	POKER	TIME	PIANO
PATERSON	SUSAN	TONGS	JOSEPH	PARIS
HIRAM	MARYLAND	FREE SPACE	CRISFIELD	BALTIMORE
KENTUCKY	TRUDY	EELGRASS	SHANTY	ESAU
SUN	KELLAMS	SALISBURY	COUNTERSPY	OYSTER

Jacob Have I Loved

JIMMY	SKIPJACK	SHADOW	WONDER	NIGHT
BRADSHAW	BUSTER	PEABODY	BOHEME	BOOMERANG
PROG	SOOK	FREE SPACE	JEAN	BLACKOUT
SPCA	RANK	JACOB	PEARL	METHODISM
TRUITT	LADIES	RASS	MAINLAND	FDR

Jacob Have I Loved

BOOMERANG	CAPTAIN	GUNNYSACK	MAINLAND	PEABODY
OYSTER	TONGS	HITLER	KELLAMS	PACIFIC
MIDWIFE	LEGACY	FREE SPACE	HIRAM	HURRICANE
SPCA	JIMMY	PAREGORIC	BALTIMORE	SHANTY
TRUITT	TIME	SEARS	JEAN	SKIPJACK

Jacob Have I Loved

WHEEZE	WONDER	LOUISE	POKER	JERGENS
PERISCOPE	CRISFIELD	TRUDY	WATERMEN	CULLING
DREDGES	BOHEME	FREE SPACE	PARIS	SABBATH
UNLIMITED	RICE	BUSTER	RASS	MOUNTAINS
JOSEPH	ESAU	PATERSON	JUILLIARD	RANK

Jacob Have I Loved

CULLING	KENTUCKY	SHADOW	CALL	WATERMEN
JEAN	SPCA	LOUISE	LEGACY	LADIES
BOHEME	ESAU	FREE SPACE	SALISBURY	CAROLINE
PERISCOPE	OYSTER	BUSTER	PEARL	PACIFIC
WHEEZE	BRADSHAW	RANK	CAPTAIN	SHANTY

Jacob Have I Loved

MAST	PROG	FERRY	SUSAN	JACOB
JUILLIARD	EELGRASS	SKIFF	BALTIMORE	PATERSON
HURRICANE	COUNTERSPY	FREE SPACE	BLACKOUT	RASS
TONGS	PEABODY	HIRAM	DREDGES	PIANO
UNLIMITED	JIMMY	NIGHT	MAINLAND	JERGENS

Jacob Have I Loved

DREDGES	MARYLAND	SUN	LADIES	LOUISE
CALL	MOUNTAINS	TRUDY	SALISBURY	SHADOW
HIRAM	PAREGORIC	FREE SPACE	FERRY	WONDER
RANK	PATERSON	WATERMEN	OYSTER	BLACKOUT
SUSAN	SKIPJACK	SEARS	JIMMY	PACIFIC

Jacob Have I Loved

MIDWIFE	BALTIMORE	CULLING	SKIFF	TONGS
MAINLAND	NIGHT	CAPTAIN	LEGACY	JERGENS
JOSEPH	BOOMERANG	FREE SPACE	GUT	KELLAMS
TRUITT	POKER	PIANO	MAST	GUNNYSACK
PEABODY	BUSTER	WHEEZE	JUILLIARD	SOOK

Jacob Have I Loved

FDR	MOUNTAINS	TRUITT	WHEEZE	LEGACY
SPCA	PATERSON	EELGRASS	MAST	COUNTERSPY
HURRICANE	SKIFF	FREE SPACE	FERRY	TIME
WATERMEN	JERGENS	SHANTY	PIANO	JIMMY
SKIPJACK	RANK	TRUDY	LOUISE	POKER

Jacob Have I Loved

BALTIMORE	KENTUCKY	SUN	NIGHT	PERISCOPE
PEARL	GUT	WONDER	SOOK	LADIES
MARYLAND	RASS	FREE SPACE	BUSTER	PROG
CAPTAIN	JACOB	PAREGORIC	CALL	METHODISM
UNLIMITED	SALISBURY	CULLING	BRADSHAW	HITLER

Jacob Have I Loved

POKER	MAST	CAPTAIN	SUN	JERGENS
COUNTERSPY	JIMMY	CRISFIELD	MARYLAND	LOUISE
OYSTER	PACIFIC	FREE SPACE	BALTIMORE	TIME
PAREGORIC	HIRAM	HITLER	JACOB	PERISCOPE
WATERMEN	RASS	HURRICANE	PEABODY	BUSTER

Jacob Have I Loved

MIDWIFE	PROG	DREDGES	RICE	PIANO
JOSEPH	GUT	EELGRASS	SALISBURY	SKIPJACK
WHEEZE	SOOK	FREE SPACE	KELLAMS	MAINLAND
NIGHT	LADIES	BRADSHAW	MOUNTAINS	PARIS
BOOMERANG	SHANTY	GUNNYSACK	TONGS	RANK

Jacob Have I Loved

PEABODY	BUSTER	PEARL	POKER	BRADSHAW
JACOB	PERISCOPE	SABBATH	MOUNTAINS	JUILLIARD
PACIFIC	LEGACY	FREE SPACE	ESAU	DREDGES
SOOK	FERRY	SUSAN	CAPTAIN	WATERMEN
GUT	KELLAMS	RANK	SALISBURY	BLACKOUT

Jacob Have I Loved

RASS	JIMMY	LADIES	FDR	GUNNYSACK
TRUDY	CULLING	KENTUCKY	CRISFIELD	JOSEPH
HITLER	PARIS	FREE SPACE	SHADOW	BOOMERANG
PATERSON	EELGRASS	WHEEZE	PIANO	MAST
TRUITT	CALL	SHANTY	BOHEME	SEARS

Jacob Have I Loved

RANK	CULLING	FDR	GUT	MOUNTAINS
SALISBURY	HURRICANE	SHANTY	TRUDY	JOSEPH
JACOB	SOOK	FREE SPACE	HITLER	CAROLINE
SABBATH	BUSTER	SPCA	SKIPJACK	MARYLAND
PERISCOPE	METHODISM	PAREGORIC	PROG	TRUITT

Jacob Have I Loved

JIMMY	CALL	CRISFIELD	JERGENS	PACIFIC
PEABODY	MIDWIFE	GUNNYSACK	UNLIMITED	LADIES
BALTIMORE	MAINLAND	FREE SPACE	WATERMEN	CAPTAIN
LOUISE	KENTUCKY	TIME	SKIFF	MAST
PARIS	KELLAMS	NIGHT	TONGS	RICE

Jacob Have I Loved

BOHEME	PACIFIC	RANK	CAROLINE	NIGHT
WHEEZE	TRUDY	SUSAN	LADIES	GUT
RASS	PEABODY	FREE SPACE	CRISFIELD	KELLAMS
MAINLAND	MAST	JERGENS	MARYLAND	DREDGES
SABBATH	BOOMERANG	TIME	SPCA	SKIFF

Jacob Have I Loved

JEAN	FERRY	PATERSON	JOSEPH	OYSTER
SHADOW	PARIS	TRUITT	EELGRASS	WONDER
WATERMEN	UNLIMITED	FREE SPACE	SHANTY	TONGS
BRADSHAW	KENTUCKY	JUILLIARD	CALL	METHODISM
LEGACY	BUSTER	HIRAM	COUNTERSPY	ESAU

Jacob Have I Loved

MARYLAND	PATERSON	TONGS	BOHEME	SKIPJACK
POKER	LOUISE	PERISCOPE	SKIFF	HIRAM
PACIFIC	CAROLINE	FREE SPACE	TIME	MAST
BALTIMORE	METHODISM	BLACKOUT	CAPTAIN	TRUITT
CRISFIELD	OYSTER	WONDER	PIANO	BUSTER

Jacob Have I Loved

JIMMY	WHEEZE	PARIS	LEGACY	BOOMERANG
LADIES	EELGRASS	MOUNTAINS	PEARL	PROG
KELLAMS	COUNTERSPY	FREE SPACE	SHANTY	SALISBURY
RASS	JEAN	BRADSHAW	CULLING	UNLIMITED
NIGHT	CALL	MAINLAND	HURRICANE	SUN

Jacob Have I Loved

KELLAMS	LEGACY	GUT	WONDER	PAREGORIC
JOSEPH	OYSTER	HURRICANE	NIGHT	CULLING
PEARL	COUNTERSPY	FREE SPACE	LADIES	SALISBURY
HIRAM	CRISFIELD	JEAN	BOOMERANG	PIANO
POKER	KENTUCKY	RASS	TONGS	JERGENS

Jacob Have I Loved

PEABODY	CALL	JIMMY	TIME	GUNNYSACK
SKIFF	TRUDY	LOUISE	PATERSON	SABBATH
BRADSHAW	JACOB	FREE SPACE	MARYLAND	RICE
METHODISM	SUSAN	CAROLINE	SEARS	HITLER
SHADOW	EELGRASS	PERISCOPE	CAPTAIN	FDR

Jacob Have I Loved

POKER	FDR	SALISBURY	LOUISE	CRISFIELD
PIANO	MAST	JOSEPH	GUT	JACOB
TRUDY	CALL	FREE SPACE	RASS	JUILLIARD
ESAU	BOHEME	TIME	METHODISM	HURRICANE
EELGRASS	HIRAM	JIMMY	TRUITT	TONGS

Jacob Have I Loved

MAINLAND	RICE	RANK	BALTIMORE	SABBATH
SHADOW	DREDGES	OYSTER	NIGHT	LADIES
COUNTERSPY	CAPTAIN	FREE SPACE	BRADSHAW	PARIS
WATERMEN	LEGACY	WHEEZE	WONDER	MIDWIFE
MARYLAND	FERRY	MOUNTAINS	SUSAN	SPCA

Jacob Have I Loved

TONGS	RANK	TIME	PEABODY	KENTUCKY
POKER	RASS	BRADSHAW	COUNTERSPY	BOOMERANG
PEARL	BLACKOUT	FREE SPACE	GUNNYSACK	CULLING
LOUISE	NIGHT	HIRAM	SHADOW	SKIPJACK
SUN	METHODISM	BOHEME	JOSEPH	TRUDY

Jacob Have I Loved

SPCA	HURRICANE	SUSAN	HITLER	FERRY
OYSTER	UNLIMITED	WONDER	CRISFIELD	SOOK
TRUITT	SABBATH	FREE SPACE	MOUNTAINS	PERISCOPE
WHEEZE	PROG	DREDGES	EELGRASS	SALISBURY
KELLAMS	SKIFF	FDR	LADIES	LEGACY

Jacob Vocabulary Word List

No.	Word	Clue/Definition
1.	ABERRATIONS	Quirks; abnormalities
2.	BEFUDDLED	Puzzled; perplexed
3.	BENEVOLENTLY	Kindly
4.	CAJOLED	Urged; appealed
5.	CONTEMPT	Dislike
6.	DELEGATION	Assigned group
7.	DELUSIONS	False beliefs or opinions
8.	DILAPIDATED	Shabby; neglected
9.	DIMINISHED	Made smaller; lessened
10.	DISCOMFITED	Frustrated
11.	DOUSE	Put out; extinguish
12.	EXASPERATED	Angered or greatly annoyed
13.	EXULTATION	Great joy
14.	FELLED	Chopped
15.	FERVENT	Having great emotion or zeal
16.	FICKLE	Changeable
17.	FUTILE	Hopeless
18.	GINGERLY	Carefully
19.	IRONY	Contrast; incongruity
20.	LITANY	Series of prayers
21.	LUGUBRIOUSLY	Mournfully; gloomily
22.	LYRICIST	One who writes words to songs
23.	MACHINATIONS	Schemes; plots
24.	MELANCHOLY	Sadness
25.	OBLIGING	Helpful
26.	OMINOUS	Threatening
27.	PARAGORIC	Opium form taken to relieve intestinal pain
28.	PETULANT	Irritable or ill-tempered
29.	PITEOUS	Pitiful; pathetic
30.	PRECARIOUS	Dangerously insecure; unstable
31.	PRETENTIOUS	Puffed-up; self-important
32.	RAMSHACKLE	Falling to ruin; tumbled-down
33.	RANKLE	Irritate or cause resentment
34.	REFURBISHED	Refinished
35.	REMONSTRANCE	Objection; protest
36.	RIVULET	Small stream
37.	SABOTEUR	One who undermines
38.	SHARDS	Fragments of a brittle substance, as of glass or metal
39.	SHRAPNEL	Shell fragments from an explosion
40.	TERRAPIN	North American aquatic turtle
41.	TORRENT	Flood; overflow
42.	TREACHEROUS	Extremely unsafe
43.	UNDAUNTED	Not discouraged or disheartened
44.	VAUDEVILLE	Stage act

Jacob Vocabulary Fill In The Blanks 1

_____ 1. Pitiful; pathetic

_____ 2. Irritate or cause resentment

_____ 3. Made smaller; lessened

_____ 4. Series of prayers

_____ 5. Contrast; incongruity

_____ 6. Refinished

_____ 7. Puffed-up; self-important

_____ 8. Falling to ruin; tumbled-down

_____ 9. Quirks; abnormalities

_____ 10. Dangerously insecure; unstable

_____ 11. Opium form taken to relieve intestinal pain

_____ 12. Shell fragments from an explosion

_____ 13. Extremely unsafe

_____ 14. Frustrated

_____ 15. Shabby; neglected

_____ 16. Stage act

_____ 17. Irritable or ill-tempered

_____ 18. Great joy

_____ 19. Not discouraged or disheartened

_____ 20. Puzzled; perplexed

Jacob Vocabulary Fill In The Blanks 1 Answer Key

PITEOUS	1. Pitiful; pathetic
RANKLE	2. Irritate or cause resentment
DIMINISHED	3. Made smaller; lessened
LITANY	4. Series of prayers
IRONY	5. Contrast; incongruity
REFURBISHED	6. Refinished
PRETENTIOUS	7. Puffed-up; self-important
RAMSHACKLE	8. Falling to ruin; tumbled-down
ABERRATIONS	9. Quirks; abnormalities
PRECARIOUS	10. Dangerously insecure; unstable
PARAGORIC	11. Opium form taken to relieve intestinal pain
SHRAPNEL	12. Shell fragments from an explosion
TREACHEROUS	13. Extremely unsafe
DISCOMFITED	14. Frustrated
DILAPIDATED	15. Shabby; neglected
VAUDEVILLE	16. Stage act
PETULANT	17. Irritable or ill-tempered
EXULTATION	18. Great joy
UNDAUNTED	19. Not discouraged or disheartened
BEFUDDLED	20. Puzzled; perplexed

Jacob Vocabulary Fill In The Blanks 2

_____ 1. Small stream

_____ 2. Stage act

_____ 3. Opium form taken to relieve intestinal pain

_____ 4. Chopped

_____ 5. Shell fragments from an explosion

_____ 6. One who undermines

_____ 7. Having great emotion or zeal

_____ 8. Objection; protest

_____ 9. Contrast; incongruity

_____ 10. Urged; appealed

_____ 11. Puffed-up; self-important

_____ 12. Irritate or cause resentment

_____ 13. Series of prayers

_____ 14. False beliefs or opinions

_____ 15. Carefully

_____ 16. Angered or greatly annoyed

_____ 17. Kindly

_____ 18. Mournfully; gloomily

_____ 19. Great joy

_____ 20. Pitiful; pathetic

Jacob Vocabulary Fill In The Blanks 2 Answer Key

RIVULET	1. Small stream
VAUDEVILLE	2. Stage act
PARAGORIC	3. Opium form taken to relieve intestinal pain
FELLED	4. Chopped
SHRAPNEL	5. Shell fragments from an explosion
SABOTEUR	6. One who undermines
FERVENT	7. Having great emotion or zeal
REMONSTRANCE	8. Objection; protest
IRONY	9. Contrast; incongruity
CAJOLED	10. Urged; appealed
PRETENTIOUS	11. Puffed-up; self-important
RANKLE	12. Irritate or cause resentment
LITANY	13. Series of prayers
DELUSIONS	14. False beliefs or opinions
GINGERLY	15. Carefully
EXASPERATED	16. Angered or greatly annoyed
BENEVOLENTLY	17. Kindly
LUGUBRIOUSLY	18. Mournfully; gloomily
EXULTATION	19. Great joy
PITEOUS	20. Pitiful; pathetic

Jacob Vocabulary Fill In The Blanks 3

_____ 1. Assigned group
_____ 2. Refinished
_____ 3. Sadness
_____ 4. Chopped
_____ 5. Hopeless
_____ 6. Irritate or cause resentment
_____ 7. Objection; protest
_____ 8. Series of prayers
_____ 9. Fragments of a brittle substance, as of glass or metal
_____ 10. Helpful
_____ 11. Made smaller; lessened
_____ 12. Having great emotion or zeal
_____ 13. Puzzled; perplexed
_____ 14. Pitiful; pathetic
_____ 15. Urged; appealed
_____ 16. Kindly
_____ 17. Threatening
_____ 18. Carefully
_____ 19. Schemes; plots
_____ 20. Shell fragments from an explosion

Jacob Vocabulary Fill In The Blanks 3 Answer Key

DELEGATION	1. Assigned group
REFURBISHED	2. Refinished
MELANCHOLY	3. Sadness
FELLED	4. Chopped
FUTILE	5. Hopeless
RANKLE	6. Irritate or cause resentment
REMONSTRANCE	7. Objection; protest
LITANY	8. Series of prayers
SHARDS	9. Fragments of a brittle substance, as of glass or metal
OBLIGING	10. Helpful
DIMINISHED	11. Made smaller; lessened
FERVENT	12. Having great emotion or zeal
BEFUDDLED	13. Puzzled; perplexed
PITEOUS	14. Pitiful; pathetic
CAJOLED	15. Urged; appealed
BENEVOLENTLY	16. Kindly
OMINOUS	17. Threatening
GINGERLY	18. Carefully
MACHINATIONS	19. Schemes; plots
SHRAPNEL	20. Shell fragments from an explosion

Jacob Vocabulary Fill In The Blanks 4

_____ 1. Hopeless

_____ 2. Falling to ruin; tumbled-down

_____ 3. One who writes words to songs

_____ 4. Small stream

_____ 5. One who undermines

_____ 6. Carefully

_____ 7. Pitiful; pathetic

_____ 8. Dangerously insecure; unstable

_____ 9. Stage act

_____ 10. Having great emotion or zeal

_____ 11. Mournfully; gloomily

_____ 12. Quirks; abnormalities

_____ 13. Dislike

_____ 14. Refinished

_____ 15. Series of prayers

_____ 16. Threatening

_____ 17. Kindly

_____ 18. Objection; protest

_____ 19. Shabby; neglected

_____ 20. Puffed-up; self-important

Jacob Vocabulary Fill In The Blanks 4 Answer Key

FUTILE	1. Hopeless
RAMSHACKLE	2. Falling to ruin; tumbled-down
LYRICIST	3. One who writes words to songs
RIVULET	4. Small stream
SABOTEUR	5. One who undermines
GINGERLY	6. Carefully
PITEOUS	7. Pitiful; pathetic
PRECARIOUS	8. Dangerously insecure; unstable
VAUDEVILLE	9. Stage act
FERVENT	10. Having great emotion or zeal
LUGUBRIOUSLY	11. Mournfully; gloomily
ABERRATIONS	12. Quirks; abnormalities
CONTEMPT	13. Dislike
REFURBISHED	14. Refinished
LITANY	15. Series of prayers
OMINOUS	16. Threatening
BENEVOLENTLY	17. Kindly
REMONSTRANCE	18. Objection; protest
DILAPIDATED	19. Shabby; neglected
PRETENTIOUS	20. Puffed-up; self-important

Jacob Vocabulary Matching 1

___ 1. LYRICIST   A. Pitiful; pathetic
___ 2. BEFUDDLED   B. Great joy
___ 3. TERRAPIN   C. False beliefs or opinions
___ 4. PITEOUS   D. Dislike
___ 5. OBLIGING   E. One who writes words to songs
___ 6. ABERRATIONS   F. Carefully
___ 7. CONTEMPT   G. Series of prayers
___ 8. FERVENT   H. Extremely unsafe
___ 9. LITANY   I. Changeable
___10. GINGERLY   J. Urged; appealed
___11. FICKLE   K. North American aquatic turtle
___12. PRECARIOUS   L. Objection; protest
___13. MACHINATIONS   M. Having great emotion or zeal
___14. FUTILE   N. Refinished
___15. REMONSTRANCE   O. Dangerously insecure; unstable
___16. SHARDS   P. Schemes; plots
___17. LUGUBRIOUSLY   Q. Mournfully; gloomily
___18. RAMSHACKLE   R. Fragments of a brittle substance, as of glass or metal
___19. TREACHEROUS   S. Irritable or ill-tempered
___20. CAJOLED   T. Quirks; abnormalities
___21. EXULTATION   U. Helpful
___22. DELUSIONS   V. Puzzled; perplexed
___23. REFURBISHED   W. Falling to ruin; tumbled-down
___24. PETULANT   X. Puffed-up; self-important
___25. PRETENTIOUS   Y. Hopeless

Jacob Vocabulary Matching 1 Answer Key

E - 1. LYRICIST		A. Pitiful; pathetic
V - 2. BEFUDDLED		B. Great joy
K - 3. TERRAPIN		C. False beliefs or opinions
A - 4. PITEOUS		D. Dislike
U - 5. OBLIGING		E. One who writes words to songs
T - 6. ABERRATIONS		F. Carefully
D - 7. CONTEMPT		G. Series of prayers
M - 8. FERVENT		H. Extremely unsafe
G - 9. LITANY		I. Changeable
F - 10. GINGERLY		J. Urged; appealed
I - 11. FICKLE		K. North American aquatic turtle
O - 12. PRECARIOUS		L. Objection; protest
P - 13. MACHINATIONS		M. Having great emotion or zeal
Y - 14. FUTILE		N. Refinished
L - 15. REMONSTRANCE		O. Dangerously insecure; unstable
R - 16. SHARDS		P. Schemes; plots
Q - 17. LUGUBRIOUSLY		Q. Mournfully; gloomily
W - 18. RAMSHACKLE		R. Fragments of a brittle substance, as of glass or metal
H - 19. TREACHEROUS		S. Irritable or ill-tempered
J - 20. CAJOLED		T. Quirks; abnormalities
B - 21. EXULTATION		U. Helpful
C - 22. DELUSIONS		V. Puzzled; perplexed
N - 23. REFURBISHED		W. Falling to ruin; tumbled-down
S - 24. PETULANT		X. Puffed-up; self-important
X - 25. PRETENTIOUS		Y. Hopeless

Jacob Vocabulary Matching 2

___ 1. SABOTEUR   A. Objection; protest
___ 2. DELEGATION   B. Falling to ruin; tumbled-down
___ 3. REFURBISHED   C. Small stream
___ 4. DOUSE   D. Extremely unsafe
___ 5. LUGUBRIOUSLY   E. Put out; extinguish
___ 6. FICKLE   F. One who undermines
___ 7. TREACHEROUS   G. Angered or greatly annoyed
___ 8. GINGERLY   H. Made smaller; lessened
___ 9. RANKLE   I. Flood; overflow
___10. CAJOLED   J. Helpful
___11. LITANY   K. Threatening
___12. DILAPIDATED   L. Irritate or cause resentment
___13. MELANCHOLY   M. Assigned group
___14. PRETENTIOUS   N. Shabby; neglected
___15. TORRENT   O. Puffed-up; self-important
___16. EXASPERATED   P. Puzzled; perplexed
___17. OBLIGING   Q. Sadness
___18. OMINOUS   R. Changeable
___19. RIVULET   S. Refinished
___20. BEFUDDLED   T. Urged; appealed
___21. IRONY   U. Mournfully; gloomily
___22. REMONSTRANCE   V. Carefully
___23. RAMSHACKLE   W. Series of prayers
___24. DIMINISHED   X. Hopeless
___25. FUTILE   Y. Contrast; incongruity

Jacob Vocabulary Matching 2 Answer Key

F - 1. SABOTEUR	A.	Objection; protest
M - 2. DELEGATION	B.	Falling to ruin; tumbled-down
S - 3. REFURBISHED	C.	Small stream
E - 4. DOUSE	D.	Extremely unsafe
U - 5. LUGUBRIOUSLY	E.	Put out; extinguish
R - 6. FICKLE	F.	One who undermines
D - 7. TREACHEROUS	G.	Angered or greatly annoyed
V - 8. GINGERLY	H.	Made smaller; lessened
L - 9. RANKLE	I.	Flood; overflow
T - 10. CAJOLED	J.	Helpful
W - 11. LITANY	K.	Threatening
N - 12. DILAPIDATED	L.	Irritate or cause resentment
Q - 13. MELANCHOLY	M.	Assigned group
O - 14. PRETENTIOUS	N.	Shabby; neglected
I - 15. TORRENT	O.	Puffed-up; self-important
G - 16. EXASPERATED	P.	Puzzled; perplexed
J - 17. OBLIGING	Q.	Sadness
K - 18. OMINOUS	R.	Changeable
C - 19. RIVULET	S.	Refinished
P - 20. BEFUDDLED	T.	Urged; appealed
Y - 21. IRONY	U.	Mournfully; gloomily
A - 22. REMONSTRANCE	V.	Carefully
B - 23. RAMSHACKLE	W.	Series of prayers
H - 24. DIMINISHED	X.	Hopeless
X - 25. FUTILE	Y.	Contrast; incongruity

Jacob Vocabulary Matching 3

___ 1. EXULTATION   A. Chopped
___ 2. RANKLE   B. Refinished
___ 3. SABOTEUR   C. Dislike
___ 4. PETULANT   D. North American aquatic turtle
___ 5. OMINOUS   E. Threatening
___ 6. REFURBISHED   F. Carefully
___ 7. PRETENTIOUS   G. Puffed-up; self-important
___ 8. DOUSE   H. Angered or greatly annoyed
___ 9. FELLED   I. One who writes words to songs
___10. LYRICIST   J. One who undermines
___11. IRONY   K. Shell fragments from an explosion
___12. EXASPERATED   L. Irritable or ill-tempered
___13. DIMINISHED   M. Helpful
___14. CONTEMPT   N. Great joy
___15. RIVULET   O. Shabby; neglected
___16. GINGERLY   P. Assigned group
___17. LITANY   Q. Irritate or cause resentment
___18. TERRAPIN   R. Put out; extinguish
___19. SHRAPNEL   S. Puzzled; perplexed
___20. BEFUDDLED   T. Not discouraged or disheartened
___21. PRECARIOUS   U. Small stream
___22. OBLIGING   V. Made smaller; lessened
___23. DELEGATION   W. Contrast; incongruity
___24. DILAPIDATED   X. Dangerously insecure; unstable
___25. UNDAUNTED   Y. Series of prayers

Jacob Vocabulary Matching 3 Answer Key

N - 1. EXULTATION		A. Chopped
Q - 2. RANKLE		B. Refinished
J - 3. SABOTEUR		C. Dislike
L - 4. PETULANT		D. North American aquatic turtle
E - 5. OMINOUS		E. Threatening
B - 6. REFURBISHED		F. Carefully
G - 7. PRETENTIOUS		G. Puffed-up; self-important
R - 8. DOUSE		H. Angered or greatly annoyed
A - 9. FELLED		I. One who writes words to songs
I - 10. LYRICIST		J. One who undermines
W - 11. IRONY		K. Shell fragments from an explosion
H - 12. EXASPERATED		L. Irritable or ill-tempered
V - 13. DIMINISHED		M. Helpful
C - 14. CONTEMPT		N. Great joy
U - 15. RIVULET		O. Shabby; neglected
F - 16. GINGERLY		P. Assigned group
Y - 17. LITANY		Q. Irritate or cause resentment
D - 18. TERRAPIN		R. Put out; extinguish
K - 19. SHRAPNEL		S. Puzzled; perplexed
S - 20. BEFUDDLED		T. Not discouraged or disheartened
X - 21. PRECARIOUS		U. Small stream
M - 22. OBLIGING		V. Made smaller; lessened
P - 23. DELEGATION		W. Contrast; incongruity
O - 24. DILAPIDATED		X. Dangerously insecure; unstable
T - 25. UNDAUNTED		Y. Series of prayers

Jacob Vocabulary Matching 4

___ 1. EXULTATION	A. Puffed-up; self-important
___ 2. DELEGATION	B. Hopeless
___ 3. ABERRATIONS	C. Great joy
___ 4. REMONSTRANCE	D. Contrast; incongruity
___ 5. GINGERLY	E. Objection; protest
___ 6. FICKLE	F. Mournfully; gloomily
___ 7. TREACHEROUS	G. Shell fragments from an explosion
___ 8. DISCOMFITED	H. Pitiful; pathetic
___ 9. FUTILE	I. Series of prayers
___10. DILAPIDATED	J. Dangerously insecure; unstable
___11. LYRICIST	K. Assigned group
___12. PRETENTIOUS	L. Falling to ruin; tumbled-down
___13. VAUDEVILLE	M. Chopped
___14. SHRAPNEL	N. One who writes words to songs
___15. IRONY	O. Shabby; neglected
___16. OMINOUS	P. Extremely unsafe
___17. PRECARIOUS	Q. Irritate or cause resentment
___18. LITANY	R. Changeable
___19. RAMSHACKLE	S. Carefully
___20. FELLED	T. Stage act
___21. LUGUBRIOUSLY	U. Irritable or ill-tempered
___22. PITEOUS	V. Frustrated
___23. PETULANT	W. Put out; extinguish
___24. DOUSE	X. Quirks; abnormalities
___25. RANKLE	Y. Threatening

Jacob Vocabulary Matching 4 Answer Key

C - 1. EXULTATION	A. Puffed-up; self-important
K - 2. DELEGATION	B. Hopeless
X - 3. ABERRATIONS	C. Great joy
E - 4. REMONSTRANCE	D. Contrast; incongruity
S - 5. GINGERLY	E. Objection; protest
R - 6. FICKLE	F. Mournfully; gloomily
P - 7. TREACHEROUS	G. Shell fragments from an explosion
V - 8. DISCOMFITED	H. Pitiful; pathetic
B - 9. FUTILE	I. Series of prayers
O - 10. DILAPIDATED	J. Dangerously insecure; unstable
N - 11. LYRICIST	K. Assigned group
A - 12. PRETENTIOUS	L. Falling to ruin; tumbled-down
T - 13. VAUDEVILLE	M. Chopped
G - 14. SHRAPNEL	N. One who writes words to songs
D - 15. IRONY	O. Shabby; neglected
Y - 16. OMINOUS	P. Extremely unsafe
J - 17. PRECARIOUS	Q. Irritate or cause resentment
I - 18. LITANY	R. Changeable
L - 19. RAMSHACKLE	S. Carefully
M - 20. FELLED	T. Stage act
F - 21. LUGUBRIOUSLY	U. Irritable or ill-tempered
H - 22. PITEOUS	V. Frustrated
U - 23. PETULANT	W. Put out; extinguish
W - 24. DOUSE	X. Quirks; abnormalities
Q - 25. RANKLE	Y. Threatening

Jacob Vocabulary Magic Squares 1

Match the definition with the vocabulary word. Put your answers in the magic squares below. When your answers are correct, all columns and rows will add to the same number.

A. EXASPERATED
B. PARAGORIC
C. PETULANT
D. PRECARIOUS
E. TORRENT
F. SHARDS
G. BEFUDDLED
H. DOUSE
I. DELUSIONS
J. TERRAPIN
K. FUTILE
L. PITEOUS
M. RAMSHACKLE
N. TREACHEROUS
O. UNDAUNTED
P. BENEVOLENTLY

1. Opium form taken to relieve intestinal pain
2. Puzzled; perplexed
3. Hopeless
4. Extremely unsafe
5. Falling to ruin; tumbled-down
6. Pitiful; pathetic
7. Put out; extinguish
8. Angered or greatly annoyed
9. Kindly
10. False beliefs or opinions
11. Flood; overflow
12. Dangerously insecure; unstable
13. Irritable or ill-tempered
14. Fragments of a brittle substance, as of glass or metal
15. North American aquatic turtle
16. Not discouraged or disheartened

A=	B=	C=	D=
E=	F=	G=	H=
I=	J=	K=	L=
M=	N=	O=	P=

Jacob Vocabulary Magic Squares 1 Answer Key

Match the definition with the vocabulary word. Put your answers in the magic squares below. When your answers are correct, all columns and rows will add to the same number.

A. EXASPERATED
B. PARAGORIC
C. PETULANT
D. PRECARIOUS
E. TORRENT
F. SHARDS
G. BEFUDDLED
H. DOUSE
I. DELUSIONS
J. TERRAPIN
K. FUTILE
L. PITEOUS
M. RAMSHACKLE
N. TREACHEROUS
O. UNDAUNTED
P. BENEVOLENTLY

1. Opium form taken to relieve intestinal pain
2. Puzzled; perplexed
3. Hopeless
4. Extremely unsafe
5. Falling to ruin; tumbled-down
6. Pitiful; pathetic
7. Put out; extinguish
8. Angered or greatly annoyed
9. Kindly
10. False beliefs or opinions
11. Flood; overflow
12. Dangerously insecure; unstable
13. Irritable or ill-tempered
14. Fragments of a brittle substance, as of glass or metal
15. North American aquatic turtle
16. Not discouraged or disheartened

A=8	B=1	C=13	D=12
E=11	F=14	G=2	H=7
I=10	J=15	K=3	L=6
M=5	N=4	O=16	P=9

Jacob Vocabulary Magic Squares 2

Match the definition with the vocabulary word. Put your answers in the magic squares below. When your answers are correct, all columns and rows will add to the same number.

A. BENEVOLENTLY
B. CAJOLED
C. MACHINATIONS
D. FERVENT
E. REMONSTRANCE
F. BEFUDDLED
G. TREACHEROUS
H. PRETENTIOUS
I. DILAPIDATED
J. CONTEMPT
K. DOUSE
L. DELEGATION
M. PETULANT
N. OMINOUS
O. EXULTATION
P. REFURBISHED

1. Threatening
2. Extremely unsafe
3. Assigned group
4. Kindly
5. Put out; extinguish
6. Urged; appealed
7. Irritable or ill-tempered
8. Puffed-up; self-important
9. Objection; protest
10. Refinished
11. Schemes; plots
12. Dislike
13. Having great emotion or zeal
14. Shabby; neglected
15. Puzzled; perplexed
16. Great joy

A=	B=	C=	D=
E=	F=	G=	H=
I=	J=	K=	L=
M=	N=	O=	P=

Jacob Vocabulary Magic Squares 2 Answer Key

Match the definition with the vocabulary word. Put your answers in the magic squares below. When your answers are correct, all columns and rows will add to the same number.

A. BENEVOLENTLY
B. CAJOLED
C. MACHINATIONS
D. FERVENT
E. REMONSTRANCE
F. BEFUDDLED
G. TREACHEROUS
H. PRETENTIOUS
I. DILAPIDATED
J. CONTEMPT
K. DOUSE
L. DELEGATION
M. PETULANT
N. OMINOUS
O. EXULTATION
P. REFURBISHED

1. Threatening
2. Extremely unsafe
3. Assigned group
4. Kindly
5. Put out; extinguish
6. Urged; appealed
7. Irritable or ill-tempered
8. Puffed-up; self-important
9. Objection; protest
10. Refinished
11. Schemes; plots
12. Dislike
13. Having great emotion or zeal
14. Shabby; neglected
15. Puzzled; perplexed
16. Great joy

A=4	B=6	C=11	D=13
E=9	F=15	G=2	H=8
I=14	J=12	K=5	L=3
M=7	N=1	O=16	P=10

Jacob Vocabulary Magic Squares 3

Match the definition with the vocabulary word. Put your answers in the magic squares below. When your answers are correct, all columns and rows will add to the same number.

A. DELUSIONS
B. LYRICIST
C. IRONY
D. MACHINATIONS
E. LITANY
F. TORRENT
G. FELLED
H. BEFUDDLED
I. TERRAPIN
J. REFURBISHED
K. DISCOMFITED
L. OMINOUS
M. REMONSTRANCE
N. PRETENTIOUS
O. EXASPERATED
P. GINGERLY

1. Angered or greatly annoyed
2. Schemes; plots
3. Refinished
4. Series of prayers
5. North American aquatic turtle
6. Flood; overflow
7. Carefully
8. Contrast; incongruity
9. Puzzled; perplexed
10. Frustrated
11. False beliefs or opinions
12. Puffed-up; self-important
13. One who writes words to songs
14. Objection; protest
15. Chopped
16. Threatening

A=	B=	C=	D=
E=	F=	G=	H=
I=	J=	K=	L=
M=	N=	O=	P=

Jacob Vocabulary Magic Squares 3 Answer Key

Match the definition with the vocabulary word. Put your answers in the magic squares below. When your answers are correct, all columns and rows will add to the same number.

A. DELUSIONS
B. LYRICIST
C. IRONY
D. MACHINATIONS
E. LITANY
F. TORRENT
G. FELLED
H. BEFUDDLED
I. TERRAPIN
J. REFURBISHED
K. DISCOMFITED
L. OMINOUS
M. REMONSTRANCE
N. PRETENTIOUS
O. EXASPERATED
P. GINGERLY

1. Angered or greatly annoyed
2. Schemes; plots
3. Refinished
4. Series of prayers
5. North American aquatic turtle
6. Flood; overflow
7. Carefully
8. Contrast; incongruity
9. Puzzled; perplexed
10. Frustrated
11. False beliefs or opinions
12. Puffed-up; self-important
13. One who writes words to songs
14. Objection; protest
15. Chopped
16. Threatening

A=11	B=13	C=8	D=2
E=4	F=6	G=15	H=9
I=5	J=3	K=10	L=16
M=14	N=12	O=1	P=7

Jacob Vocabulary Magic Squares 4

Match the definition with the vocabulary word. Put your answers in the magic squares below. When your answers are correct, all columns and rows will add to the same number.

A. MELANCHOLY
B. TREACHEROUS
C. EXULTATION
D. MACHINATIONS
E. SABOTEUR
F. CONTEMPT
G. GINGERLY
H. IRONY
I. FELLED
J. DIMINISHED
K. BEFUDDLED
L. RIVULET
M. OMINOUS
N. REMONSTRANCE
O. VAUDEVILLE
P. PITEOUS

1. Contrast; incongruity
2. Threatening
3. Extremely unsafe
4. Puzzled; perplexed
5. Made smaller; lessened
6. Great joy
7. Pitiful; pathetic
8. One who undermines
9. Stage act
10. Dislike
11. Chopped
12. Schemes; plots
13. Sadness
14. Small stream
15. Carefully
16. Objection; protest

A=	B=	C=	D=
E=	F=	G=	H=
I=	J=	K=	L=
M=	N=	O=	P=

Jacob Vocabulary Magic Squares 4 Answer Key

Match the definition with the vocabulary word. Put your answers in the magic squares below. When your answers are correct, all columns and rows will add to the same number.

A. MELANCHOLY
B. TREACHEROUS
C. EXULTATION
D. MACHINATIONS
E. SABOTEUR
F. CONTEMPT
G. GINGERLY
H. IRONY
I. FELLED
J. DIMINISHED
K. BEFUDDLED
L. RIVULET
M. OMINOUS
N. REMONSTRANCE
O. VAUDEVILLE
P. PITEOUS

1. Contrast; incongruity
2. Threatening
3. Extremely unsafe
4. Puzzled; perplexed
5. Made smaller; lessened
6. Great joy
7. Pitiful; pathetic
8. One who undermines
9. Stage act
10. Dislike
11. Chopped
12. Schemes; plots
13. Sadness
14. Small stream
15. Carefully
16. Objection; protest

A=13	B=3	C=6	D=12
E=8	F=10	G=15	H=1
I=11	J=5	K=4	L=14
M=2	N=16	O=9	P=7

Jacob Vocabulary Word Search 1

Words are placed backwards, forward, diagonally, up and down. Clues listed below can help you find the words. Circle the hidden vocabulary words in the maze.

```
F U T I L E L T O R R E N T P D D C F W
Y E R B L G E Y M Y C L B R R E I A I M
L Q R D B L L Z G O V Z Y E E L M J C H
Y Q Q V U R P F N Y H S Z A C U I O K V
C L G V E P I T E O U S K C A S N L L G
S Y I G M N E O V L G X E H R I I E E Y
L R N Z D M T H M N L X B E I O S D A P
U I G M P I S B I I A E P R O N H Z B F
G C Q T J D L G P S N M D O U S E P E V
U I C S R T I A P N F O F U S H D A R M
B S Q A M L E E P O V S U S N E G R R Q
R T H B B G R R L I Z A H S H V B A A S
I S X O Y A A E R T D V U S L E Y G T C
O S T T T J N S Y A L A I D F Z N O I X
U D Y E N P K T R T P B T U E L A R O S
S Q D U A Y L M P L R I D E D V T I N P
L J D R W D E T N U A D N U D D I C S T
Y R H B W S K P F X L D G T D R L L R D
W S W M U B D E L E G A T I O N W X L N
Z Q C O V L R B D M E L A N C H O L Y E
J G D P E T U L A N T J Y G Z W N J C X
```

Angered or greatly annoyed (11)
Assigned group (10)
Carefully (8)
Changeable (6)
Chopped (6)
Contrast; incongruity (5)
Dangerously insecure; unstable (10)
Dislike (8)
Extremely unsafe (11)
False beliefs or opinions (9)
Flood; overflow (7)
Fragments of a brittle substance, as of glass or metal (6)
Great joy (10)
Having great emotion or zeal (7)
Helpful (8)
Hopeless (6)
Irritable or ill-tempered (8)
Irritate or cause resentment (6)
Made smaller; lessened (10)

Mournfully; gloomily (12)
North American aquatic turtle (8)
Not discouraged or disheartened (9)
One who undermines (8)
One who writes words to songs (8)
Opium form taken to relieve intestinal pain (9)
Pitiful; pathetic (7)
Put out; extinguish (5)
Puzzled; perplexed (9)
Quirks; abnormalities (11)
Refinished (11)
Sadness (10)
Series of prayers (6)
Shabby; neglected (11)
Shell fragments from an explosion (8)
Small stream (7)
Stage act (10)
Threatening (7)
Urged; appealed (7)

Jacob Vocabulary Word Search 1 Answer Key

Words are placed backwards, forward, diagonally, up and down. Clues listed below can help you find the words. Circle the hidden vocabulary words in the maze.

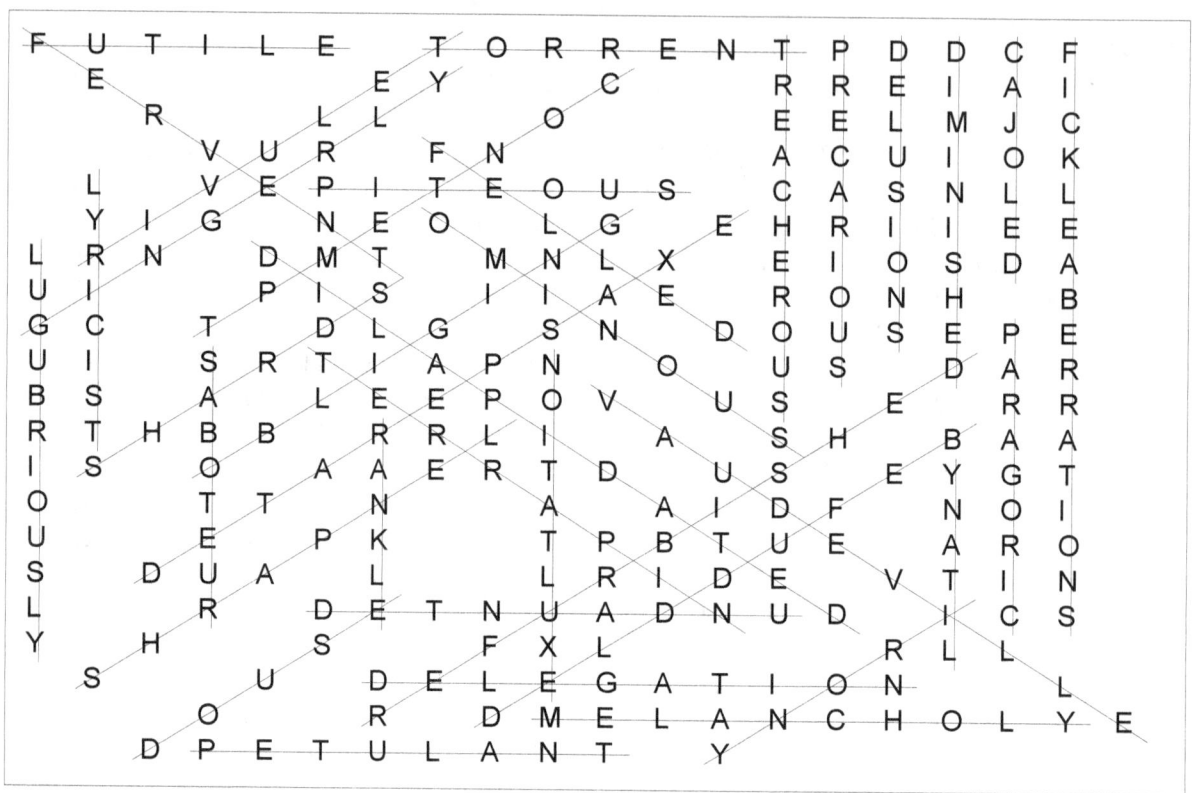

Angered or greatly annoyed (11)
Assigned group (10)
Carefully (8)
Changeable (6)
Chopped (6)
Contrast; incongruity (5)
Dangerously insecure; unstable (10)
Dislike (8)
Extremely unsafe (11)
False beliefs or opinions (9)
Flood; overflow (7)
Fragments of a brittle substance, as of glass or metal (6)
Great joy (10)
Having great emotion or zeal (7)
Helpful (8)
Hopeless (6)
Irritable or ill-tempered (8)
Irritate or cause resentment (6)
Made smaller; lessened (10)
Mournfully; gloomily (12)
North American aquatic turtle (8)
Not discouraged or disheartened (9)
One who undermines (8)
One who writes words to songs (8)
Opium form taken to relieve intestinal pain (9)
Pitiful; pathetic (7)
Put out; extinguish (5)
Puzzled; perplexed (9)
Quirks; abnormalities (11)
Refinished (11)
Sadness (10)
Series of prayers (6)
Shabby; neglected (11)
Shell fragments from an explosion (8)
Small stream (7)
Stage act (10)
Threatening (7)
Urged; appealed (7)

Jacob Vocabulary Word Search 2

Words are placed backwards, forward, diagonally, up and down. Clues listed below can help you find the words. Circle the hidden vocabulary words in the maze.

```
O B L I G I N G D E T A D I P A L I D Y
P U N D A U N T E D D G F C A J O L E D
R X D T J S Q L D E H S I B R U F E R Z
E X D R C F F X M W T Q C R A X D W S H
C Z B I Z Q U T H R N W K M G V P T H R
A H X F M C Z T J Y E Z L D O C V D A R
R P X D R I F H I G V C E Y R R I J R T
I T M L P M N F C L R L R N I S N R D Y
O V A U D E V I L L E Q I B C D O U S E
U L D G B L T J S N F P V O O E I E U S
S Y E U P A P U P H A M M Z M L T T O F
L R L B V N B A L R E F N T I L A O R S
Q I U R G C R E R A I D S S N E T B E D
G C S I K H V E R T N S U T O F L A H S
I I I O S O T B E R S T O M U D U S C Q
N S O U D L R D E T A R E P S A X E A S
G T N S M Y A C L S R T T I J K E R E Q
E T S L M M N F M E G S I Y R Z X Z R L
R C V Y L F K B N P N F P O P O R F T P
L I T A N Y L T E L U V I R N N N R W K
Y Z Y L T N E L O V E N E B Y S Q Y Y X
```

Angered or greatly annoyed (11)
Carefully (8)
Changeable (6)
Chopped (6)
Contrast; incongruity (5)
Dangerously insecure; unstable (10)
Extremely unsafe (11)
False beliefs or opinions (9)
Flood; overflow (7)
Fragments of a brittle substance, as of glass or metal (6)
Frustrated (11)
Great joy (10)
Having great emotion or zeal (7)
Helpful (8)
Hopeless (6)
Irritable or ill-tempered (8)
Irritate or cause resentment (6)
Kindly (12)
Made smaller; lessened (10)
Mournfully; gloomily (12)
North American aquatic turtle (8)
Not discouraged or disheartened (9)
One who undermines (8)
One who writes words to songs (8)
Opium form taken to relieve intestinal pain (9)
Pitiful; pathetic (7)
Put out; extinguish (5)
Quirks; abnormalities (11)
Refinished (11)
Sadness (10)
Series of prayers (6)
Shabby; neglected (11)
Shell fragments from an explosion (8)
Small stream (7)
Stage act (10)
Threatening (7)
Urged; appealed (7)

Jacob Vocabulary Word Search 2 Answer Key

Words are placed backwards, forward, diagonally, up and down. Clues listed below can help you find the words. Circle the hidden vocabulary words in the maze.

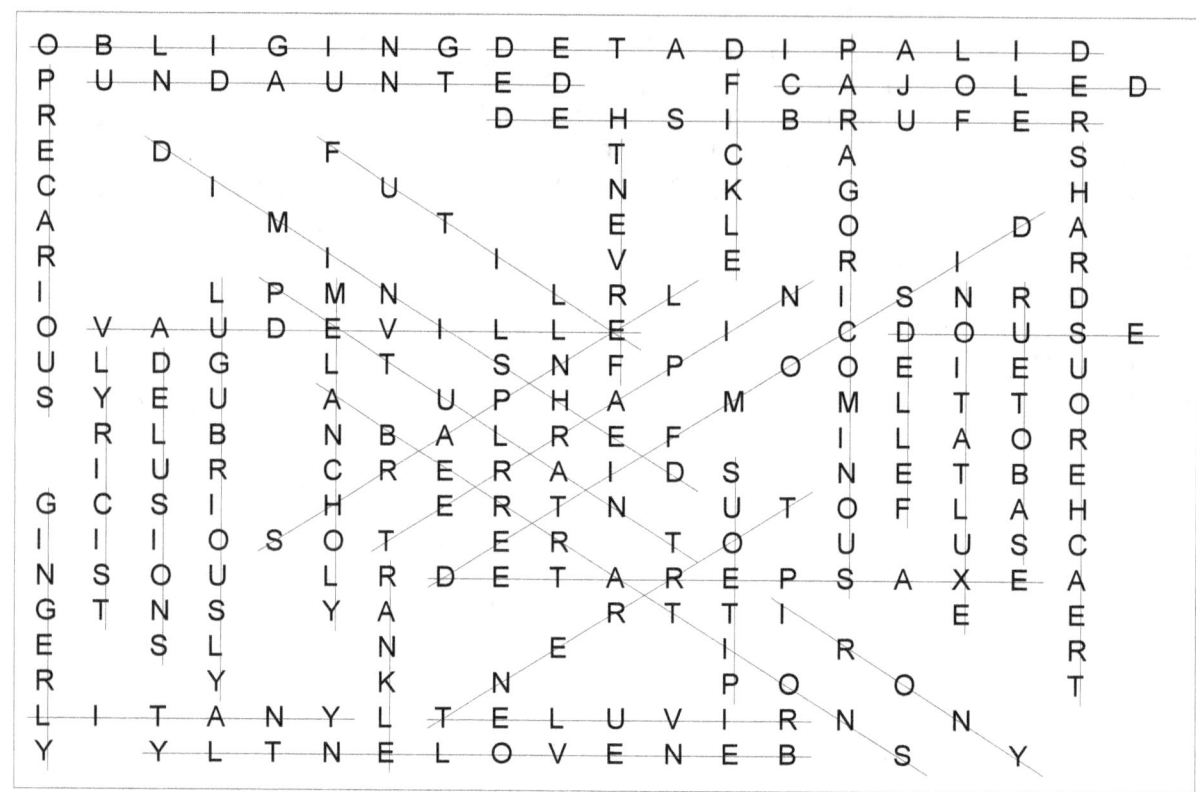

Angered or greatly annoyed (11)
Carefully (8)
Changeable (6)
Chopped (6)
Contrast; incongruity (5)
Dangerously insecure; unstable (10)
Extremely unsafe (11)
False beliefs or opinions (9)
Flood; overflow (7)
Fragments of a brittle substance, as of glass or metal (6)
Frustrated (11)
Great joy (10)
Having great emotion or zeal (7)
Helpful (8)
Hopeless (6)
Irritable or ill-tempered (8)
Irritate or cause resentment (6)
Kindly (12)
Made smaller; lessened (10)

Mournfully; gloomily (12)
North American aquatic turtle (8)
Not discouraged or disheartened (9)
One who undermines (8)
One who writes words to songs (8)
Opium form taken to relieve intestinal pain (9)
Pitiful; pathetic (7)
Put out; extinguish (5)
Quirks; abnormalities (11)
Refinished (11)
Sadness (10)
Series of prayers (6)
Shabby; neglected (11)
Shell fragments from an explosion (8)
Small stream (7)
Stage act (10)
Threatening (7)
Urged; appealed (7)

Jacob Vocabulary Word Search 3

Words are placed backwards, forward, diagonally, up and down. Words listed below are included in the maze. Circle the hidden vocabulary words in the maze.

```
V B D F T O R R E N T L E F D L R R F G
A E D F V E N D C P E I X I E U A E E W
U N F R W T R Q M N H T A C L G N M R D
D E E E K W R R P N P A S K E U K O V M
E V X R L H Z A A D C N P L G B L N E P
V O U Z Q L R G E P D Y E E A R E S N N
I L L Z L H E L W R I G R L T I V T T Z
L E T S S T O D S B L N A K I O C R R N
L N A R H J V A Q E A I T C O U J A E J
E T T M A A B Y H F P G E A N S F N A S
M L I C X O R H P U I I D H F L T C C C
A Y O D T C L D J D D L K S B Y Y E H D
C P N E I Y Y Y S D A B C M Y P Z N E S
H A U Q T M R Z X L T O P A P D Z G R Q
I R Q Q F T I Y X E E G P R F D R R O H
N A C P Y N C N S D D V R X Y E R S U Y
A G W C K A I T I V W G L Y T P N S Y
T O I D Z L S C H S N W O T J N I M P R
I R Z N Z U T F R N H T P X U T R H Q
O I X P G T Q U F Z C E N M L A E I D D
N C M Z R E S T S N I S D E D D O V O T
S M H W K P R I A H R Y F T S N U U F Q
N S N O I S U L E D O M I N O U S L M M
G B M L M S E E Y X N V N O S E R E C J
P P F X Y M H J H D Y J Q C S G H T F P
```

BEFUDDLED   EXULTATION   MACHINATIONS   RIVULET

BENEVOLENTLY   FELLED   MELANCHOLY   SABOTEUR

CAJOLED   FERVENT   OBLIGING   SHARDS

CONTEMPT   FICKLE   OMINOUS   SHRAPNEL

DELEGATION   FUTILE   PARAGORIC   TERRAPIN

DELUSIONS   GINGERLY   PETULANT   TORRENT

DILAPIDATED   IRONY   PITEOUS   TREACHEROUS

DIMINISHED   LITANY   RAMSHACKLE   UNDAUNTED

DOUSE   LUGUBRIOUSLY   RANKLE   VAUDEVILLE

EXASPERATED   LYRICIST   REMONSTRANCE

Jacob Vocabulary Word Search 3 Answer Key

Words are placed backwards, forward, diagonally, up and down. Words listed below are included in the maze. Circle the hidden vocabulary words in the maze.

BEFUDDLED	EXULTATION	MACHINATIONS	RIVULET
BENEVOLENTLY	FELLED	MELANCHOLY	SABOTEUR
CAJOLED	FERVENT	OBLIGING	SHARDS
CONTEMPT	FICKLE	OMINOUS	SHRAPNEL
DELEGATION	FUTILE	PARAGORIC	TERRAPIN
DELUSIONS	GINGERLY	PETULANT	TORRENT
DILAPIDATED	IRONY	PITEOUS	TREACHEROUS
DIMINISHED	LITANY	RAMSHACKLE	UNDAUNTED
DOUSE	LUGUBRIOUSLY	RANKLE	VAUDEVILLE
EXASPERATED	LYRICIST	REMONSTRANCE	

Jacob Vocabulary Word Search 4

Words are placed backwards, forward, diagonally, up and down. Words listed below are included in the maze. Circle the hidden vocabulary words in the maze.

```
S A B O T E U R A M S H A C K L E T P F
U U D D W B P C S U N K T A M S B R R T
O N I P P G L R O P O P F J U N E E E Z
I D S O R N I E T N I H N O V O N A C C
T A C L M O T N H X T D D L W I E C A K
N U O B H I A Q G P A E N E G T V H R B
E N M E P T N M G E R F M D B A O E I Y
T T F L C A Y O B P R E F P Q N L R O F
E E I L Q T G E U M E L Y C T I E O U M
R D T I J L F N S S B L Y F M H N U S Z
P M E V T U K P Y H A E Y E Q C T S P R
M E D E D X G Z A A R D H R C A L R Z Z
D E T D V E W J B R Z A N V I M Y W B P
T R L U E P X M A H S X G C N V C N Y V G
J E D A L L G A H S X G C N V Y I F B H
D F E V N A U Z S Q F N O T E X C S J F
B X H H C C N S R P A W R R F L X N T F
Z X S C C Z H T I R E V F N I R L V U K
G N I G I L B O T O T R I M C C T T I V
C K B Y F P Z S L K N P A C K R I R R G
K G R J P K N P C Y A S V T L L T A O P
B N U G T O M J W R I V U L E T Z N N X
L C F N M N B P R B G L C D Q D F K Y W
K K E E Z T D E H S I N I M I D Y L R V
T O R R E N T T R D I L A P I D A T E D G
```

ABERRATIONS	EXULTATION	OBLIGING	RIVULET
BEFUDDLED	FELLED	OMINOUS	SABOTEUR
BENEVOLENTLY	FERVENT	PARAGORIC	SHARDS
CAJOLED	FICKLE	PETULANT	SHRAPNEL
CONTEMPT	FUTILE	PITEOUS	TERRAPIN
DELUSIONS	GINGERLY	PRECARIOUS	TORRENT
DILAPIDATED	IRONY	PRETENTIOUS	TREACHEROUS
DIMINISHED	LITANY	RAMSHACKLE	UNDAUNTED
DISCOMFITED	LYRICIST	RANKLE	VAUDEVILLE
DOUSE	MACHINATIONS	REFURBISHED	
EXASPERATED	MELANCHOLY	REMONSTRANCE	

Jacob Vocabulary Word Search 4 Answer Key

Words are placed backwards, forward, diagonally, up and down. Words listed below are included in the maze. Circle the hidden vocabulary words in the maze.

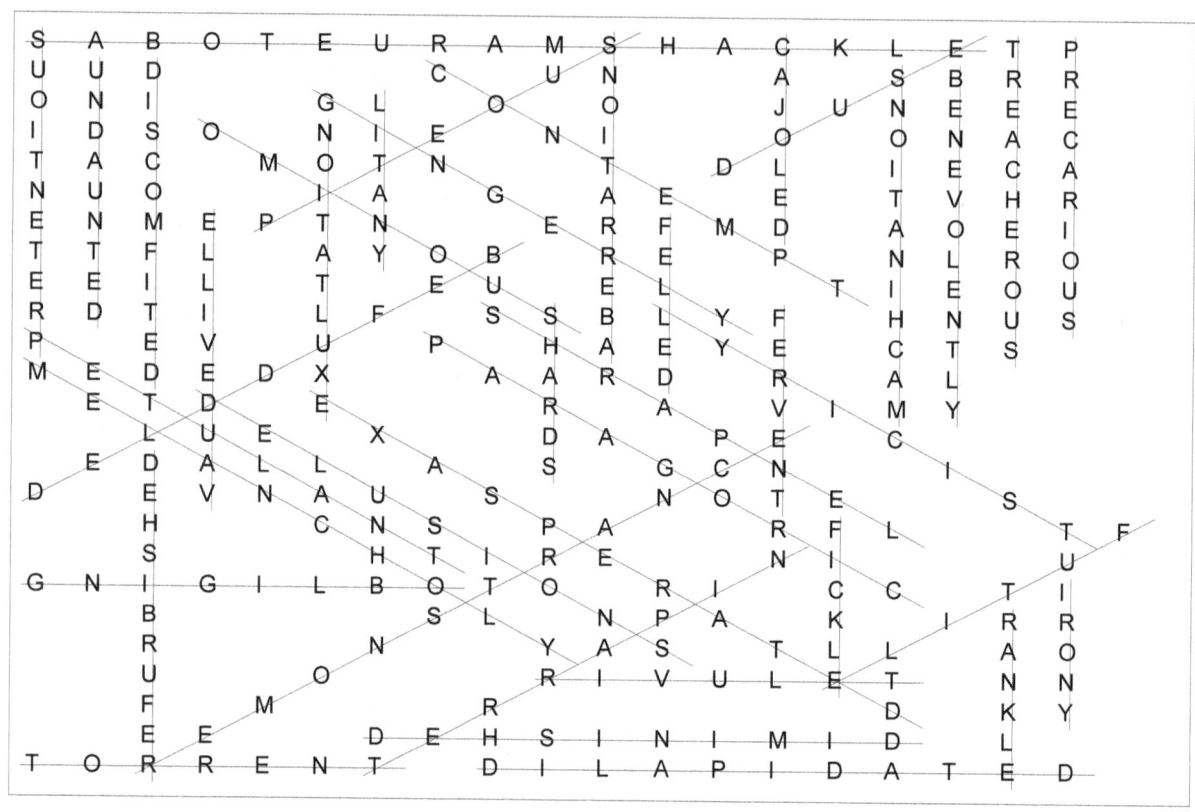

ABERRATIONS	EXULTATION	OBLIGING	RIVULET
BEFUDDLED	FELLED	OMINOUS	SABOTEUR
BENEVOLENTLY	FERVENT	PARAGORIC	SHARDS
CAJOLED	FICKLE	PETULANT	SHRAPNEL
CONTEMPT	FUTILE	PITEOUS	TERRAPIN
DELUSIONS	GINGERLY	PRECARIOUS	TORRENT
DILAPIDATED	IRONY	PRETENTIOUS	TREACHEROUS
DIMINISHED	LITANY	RAMSHACKLE	UNDAUNTED
DISCOMFITED	LYRICIST	RANKLE	VAUDEVILLE
DOUSE	MACHINATIONS	REFURBISHED	
EXASPERATED	MELANCHOLY	REMONSTRANCE	

Jacob Vocabulary Crossword 1

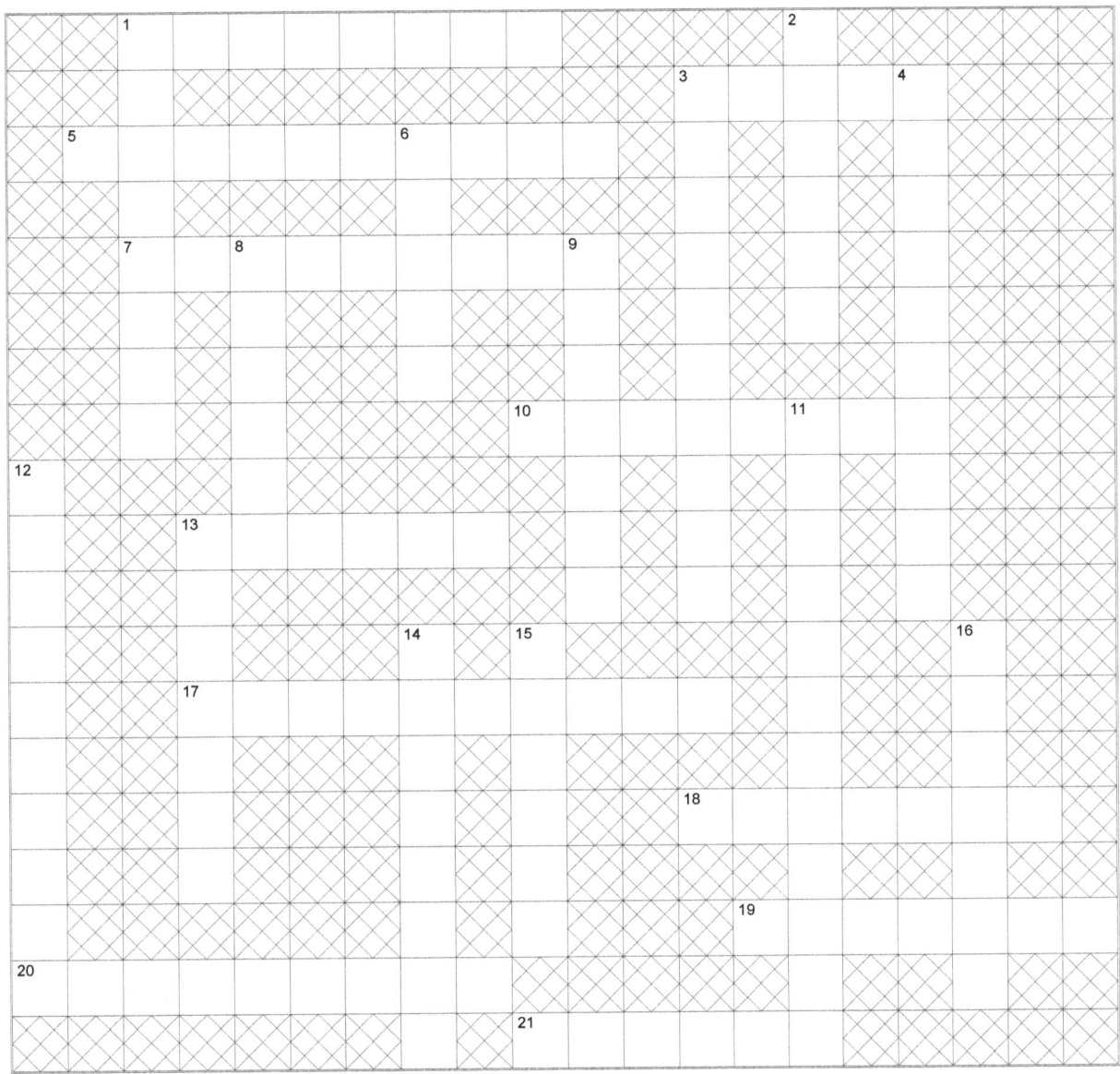

Across
1. One who undermines
3. Put out; extinguish
5. Dangerously insecure; unstable
7. Opium form taken to relieve intestinal pain
10. Dislike
13. Chopped
17. Stage act
18. Pitiful; pathetic
19. Flood; overflow
20. False beliefs or opinions
21. Fragments of a brittle substance, as of glass or metal

Down
1. Shell fragments from an explosion
2. Hopeless
3. Assigned group
4. Great joy
6. Contrast; incongruity
8. Irritate or cause resentment
9. Urged; appealed
11. Schemes; plots
12. Made smaller; lessened
13. Having great emotion or zeal
14. Irritable or ill-tempered
15. Series of prayers
16. Small stream

Jacob Vocabulary Crossword 1 Answer Key

	1 S	A	B	O	T	E	U	R			2 F		
	H								3 D	O	U	S	4 E
5 P	R	E	C	A	R	6 I	O	U	S	E		T	X
	A					R			L			I	U
	7 P	A	8 R	A	G	O	R	I	9 C	E		L	L
	N		A			N			A	G		E	T
	E		N			Y		10 C	O	N	T	E	M	P	T
	L		K						L		I		A		I
12 D			L						E		O		C		O
I	13 F	E	L	L	E	D			E				H		N
M	E				14 P		15 L		D		N				
I	R										I		16 R
N	17 V	A	U	D	E	V	I	L	L	E			I
I	E				T		T				N		V
S	N				U		A		18 P	I	T	E	O	U	S
H	T				L		N		I				L
E					A		Y		19 T	O	R	R	E	N	T
20 D	E	L	U	S	I	O	N	S	N				T
					21 T		S	H	A	R	D	S

Across
1. One who undermines
3. Put out; extinguish
5. Dangerously insecure; unstable
7. Opium form taken to relieve intestinal pain
10. Dislike
13. Chopped
17. Stage act
18. Pitiful; pathetic
19. Flood; overflow
20. False beliefs or opinions
21. Fragments of a brittle substance, as of glass or metal

Down
1. Shell fragments from an explosion
2. Hopeless
3. Assigned group
4. Great joy
6. Contrast; incongruity
8. Irritate or cause resentment
9. Urged; appealed
11. Schemes; plots
12. Made smaller; lessened
13. Having great emotion or zeal
14. Irritable or ill-tempered
15. Series of prayers
16. Small stream

Jacob Vocabulary Crossword 2

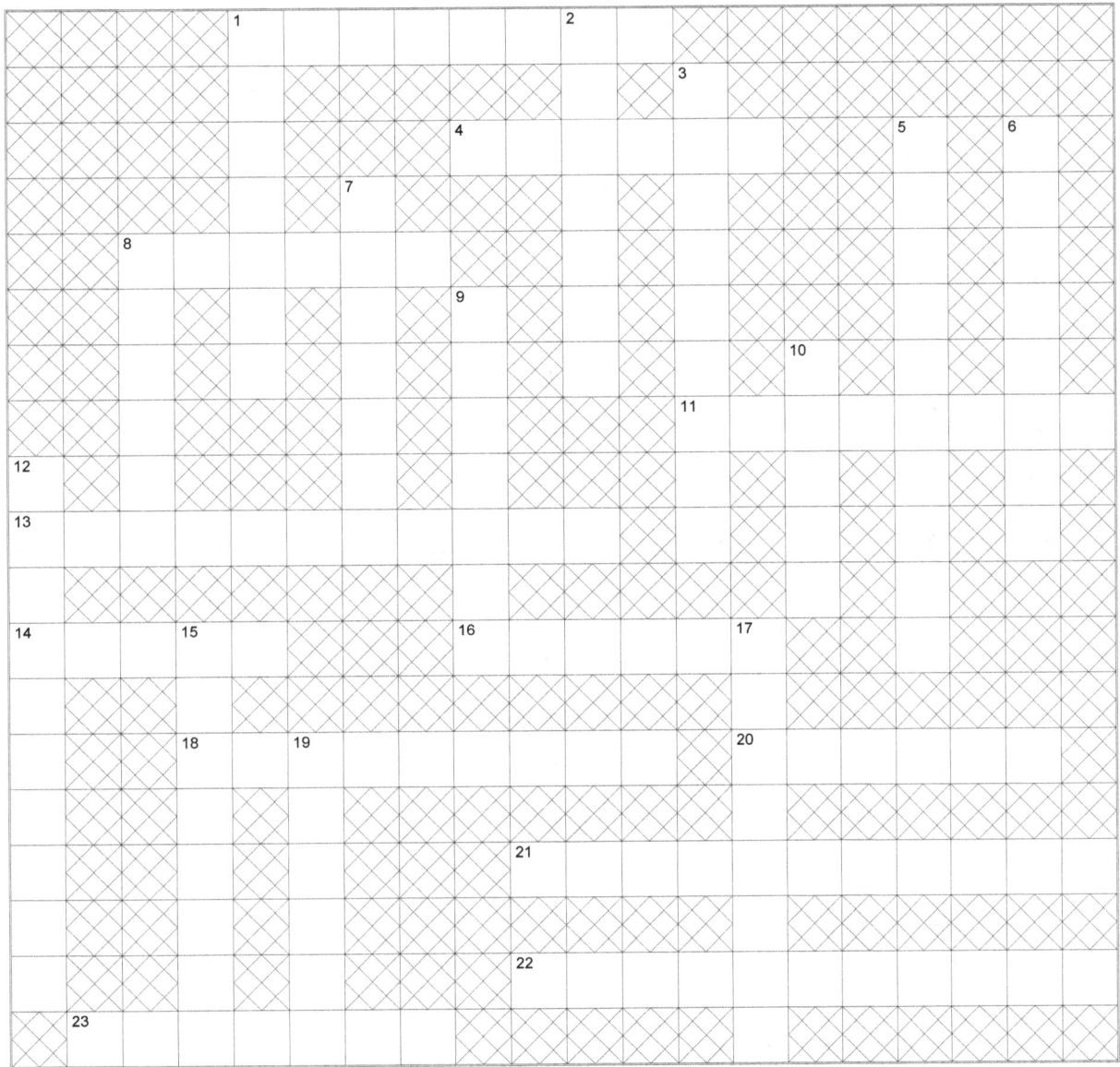

Across
1. Dislike
4. Series of prayers
8. Chopped
11. North American aquatic turtle
13. Quirks; abnormalities
14. Put out; extinguish
16. Fragments of a brittle substance, as of glass or metal
18. Puzzled; perplexed
20. Irritate or cause resentment
21. Angered or greatly annoyed
22. Puffed-up; self-important
23. Flood; overflow

Down
1. Urged; appealed
2. Pitiful; pathetic
3. Not discouraged or disheartened
5. Assigned group
6. Helpful
7. Having great emotion or zeal
8. Hopeless
9. Threatening
10. Contrast; incongruity
12. Stage act
15. One who undermines
17. Shell fragments from an explosion
19. Changeable

Jacob Vocabulary Crossword 2 Answer Key

Across
1. Dislike
4. Series of prayers
8. Chopped
11. North American aquatic turtle
13. Quirks; abnormalities
14. Put out; extinguish
16. Fragments of a brittle substance, as of glass or metal
18. Puzzled; perplexed
20. Irritate or cause resentment
21. Angered or greatly annoyed
22. Puffed-up; self-important
23. Flood; overflow

Down
1. Urged; appealed
2. Pitiful; pathetic
3. Not discouraged or disheartened
5. Assigned group
6. Helpful
7. Having great emotion or zeal
8. Hopeless
9. Threatening
10. Contrast; incongruity
12. Stage act
15. One who undermines
17. Shell fragments from an explosion
19. Changeable

Jacob Vocabulary Crossword 3

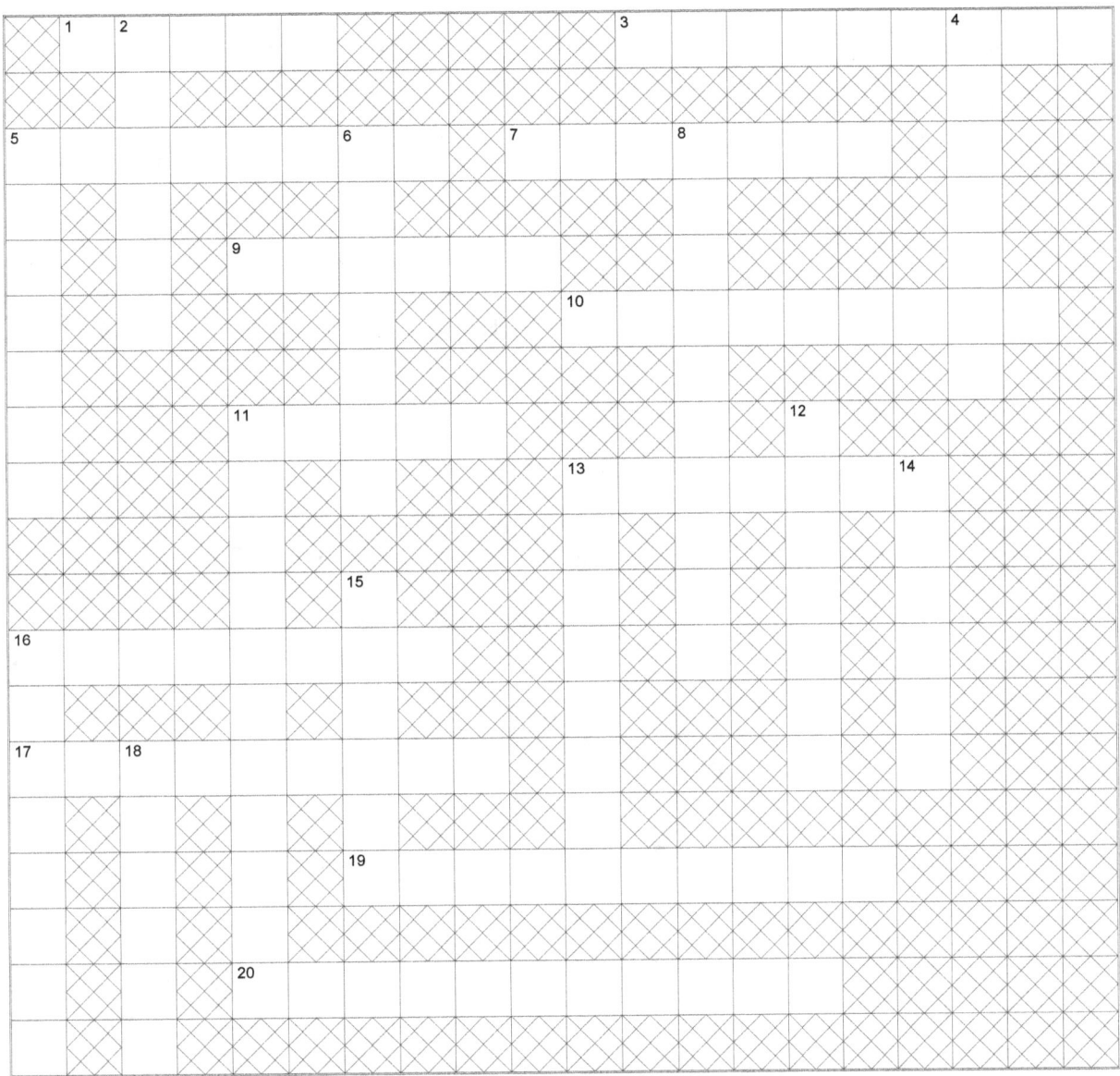

Across
1. Contrast; incongruity
3. Opium form taken to relieve intestinal pain
5. Dislike
7. Having great emotion or zeal
9. Series of prayers
10. Not discouraged or disheartened
11. Put out; extinguish
13. Threatening
16. Shell fragments from an explosion
17. Puzzled; perplexed
19. Assigned group
20. Frustrated

Down
2. Irritate or cause resentment
4. Small stream
5. Urged; appealed
6. Pitiful; pathetic
8. Stage act
11. Shabby; neglected
12. Flood; overflow
13. Helpful
14. Fragments of a brittle substance, as of glass or metal
15. Chopped
16. One who undermines
18. Hopeless

Jacob Vocabulary Crossword 3 Answer Key

Across
1. Contrast; incongruity
3. Opium form taken to relieve intestinal pain
5. Dislike
7. Having great emotion or zeal
9. Series of prayers
10. Not discouraged or disheartened
11. Put out; extinguish
13. Threatening
16. Shell fragments from an explosion
17. Puzzled; perplexed
19. Assigned group
20. Frustrated

Down
2. Irritate or cause resentment
4. Small stream
5. Urged; appealed
6. Pitiful; pathetic
8. Stage act
11. Shabby; neglected
12. Flood; overflow
13. Helpful
14. Fragments of a brittle substance, as of glass or metal
15. Chopped
16. One who undermines
18. Hopeless

Jacob Vocabulary Crossword 4

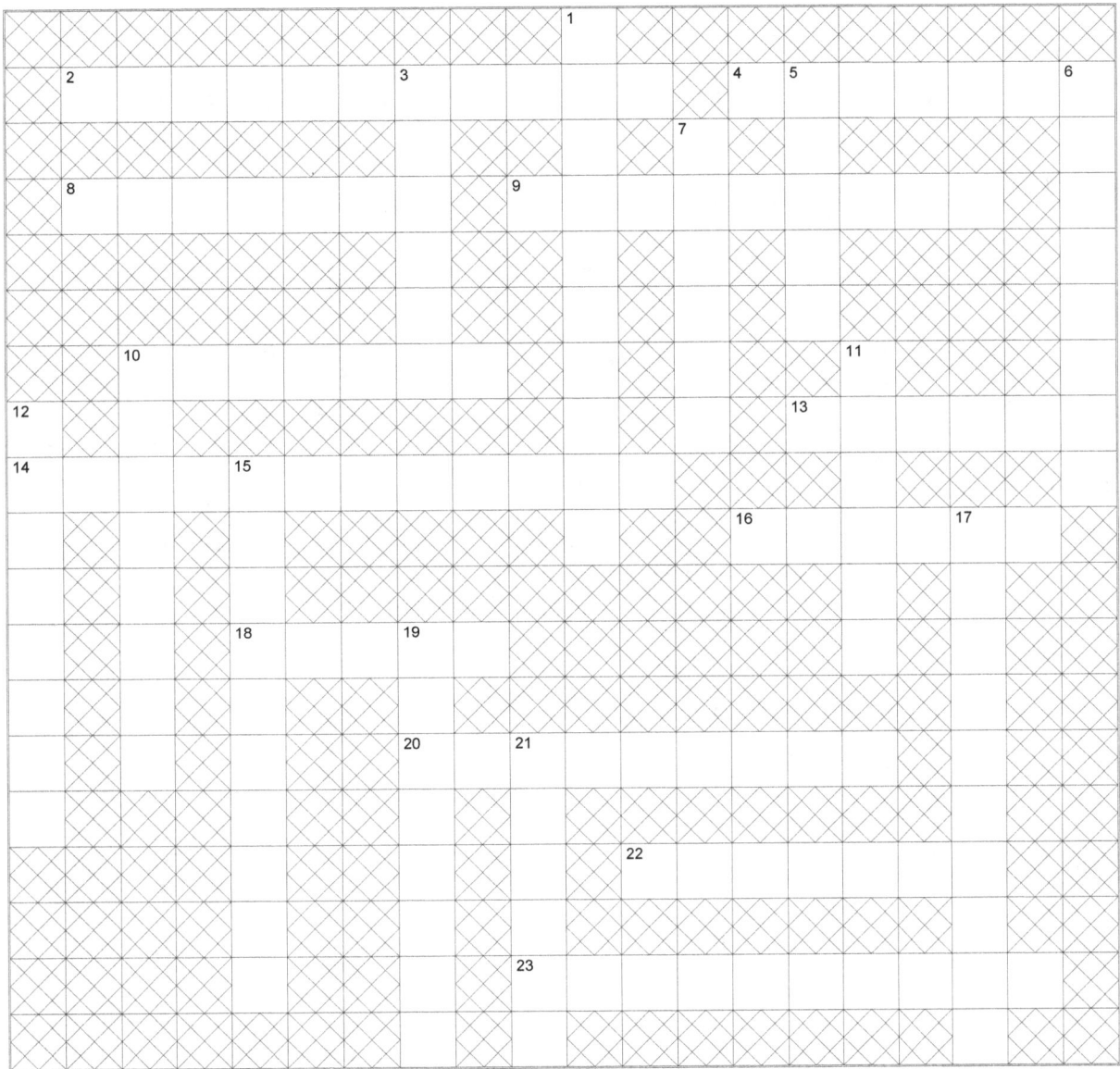

Across
2. Frustrated
4. Pitiful; pathetic
8. Having great emotion or zeal
9. Opium form taken to relieve intestinal pain
10. Urged; appealed
13. Changeable
14. Kindly
16. Fragments of a brittle substance, as of glass or metal
18. Put out; extinguish
20. Puzzled; perplexed
22. Small stream
23. Great joy

Down
1. Sadness
3. Hopeless
5. Contrast; incongruity
6. Shell fragments from an explosion
7. Irritate or cause resentment
10. Dislike
11. Series of prayers
12. Helpful
15. Stage act
17. Assigned group
19. One who undermines
21. Chopped

Jacob Vocabulary Crossword 4 Answer Key

Across
2. Frustrated
4. Pitiful; pathetic
8. Having great emotion or zeal
9. Opium form taken to relieve intestinal pain
10. Urged; appealed
13. Changeable
14. Kindly
16. Fragments of a brittle substance, as of glass or metal
18. Put out; extinguish
20. Puzzled; perplexed
22. Small stream
23. Great joy

Down
1. Sadness
3. Hopeless
5. Contrast; incongruity
6. Shell fragments from an explosion
7. Irritate or cause resentment
10. Dislike
11. Series of prayers
12. Helpful
15. Stage act
17. Assigned group
19. One who undermines
21. Chopped

Jacob Vocabulary Juggle Letters 1

1. TETAOILXNU = 1. _____
   Great joy

2. EMNOCYALHL = 2. _____
   Sadness

3. SMDEIFICDOT = 3. _____
   Frustrated

4. KLFECI = 4. _____
   Changeable

5. TPURISNEEOT = 5. _____
   Puffed-up; self-important

6. DACEOLJ = 6. _____
   Urged; appealed

7. RTANEONMCRSE = 7. _____
   Objection; protest

8. TRONRTE = 8. _____
   Flood; overflow

9. GSLUURBYOUIL = 9. _____
   Mournfully; gloomily

10. LTEYOVLEENBN =10. _____
    Kindly

11. OUESD =11. _____
    Put out; extinguish

12. BRSATUEO =12. _____
    One who undermines

13. LVEIEVUADL =13. _____
    Stage act

14. SEOPIUT =14. _____
    Pitiful; pathetic

15. HSEURETROAC =15. _____
    Extremely unsafe

Jacob Vocabulary Juggle Letters 1 Answer Key

1. TETAOILXNU = 1. EXULTATION
Great joy

2. EMNOCYALHL = 2. MELANCHOLY
Sadness

3. SMDEIFICDOT = 3. DISCOMFITED
Frustrated

4. KLFECI = 4. FICKLE
Changeable

5. TPURISNEEOT = 5. PRETENTIOUS
Puffed-up; self-important

6. DACEOLJ = 6. CAJOLED
Urged; appealed

7. RTANEONMCRSE = 7. REMONSTRANCE
Objection; protest

8. TRONRTE = 8. TORRENT
Flood; overflow

9. GSLUURBYOUIL = 9. LUGUBRIOUSLY
Mournfully; gloomily

10. LTEYOVLEENBN =10. BENEVOLENTLY
Kindly

11. OUESD =11. DOUSE
Put out; extinguish

12. BRSATUEO =12. SABOTEUR
One who undermines

13. LVEIEVUADL =13. VAUDEVILLE
Stage act

14. SEOPIUT =14. PITEOUS
Pitiful; pathetic

15. HSEURETROAC =15. TREACHEROUS
Extremely unsafe

Jacob Vocabulary Juggle Letters 2

1. USTPOIE = 1. _____
   Pitiful; pathetic

2. YLSUGURULOBI = 2. _____
   Mournfully; gloomily

3. ERNLKA = 3. _____
   Irritate or cause resentment

4. EIATPRRN = 4. _____
   North American aquatic turtle

5. FEUEBLDDD = 5. _____
   Puzzled; perplexed

6. OINSDSLUE = 6. _____
   False beliefs or opinions

7. UFTELI = 7. _____
   Hopeless

8. TERSPTOIENU = 8. _____
   Puffed-up; self-important

9. GILEYNGR = 9. _____
   Carefully

10. XEEEDTPARAS = 10. _____
    Angered or greatly annoyed

11. UOONISM = 11. _____
    Threatening

12. ILUEAVVDLE = 12. _____
    Stage act

13. BINGOIGL = 13. _____
    Helpful

14. PIEADIDTLDA = 14. _____
    Shabby; neglected

15. NAGEDLOTEI = 15. _____
    Assigned group

Jacob Vocabulary Juggle Letters 2 Answer Key

1. USTPOIE = 1. PITEOUS
Pitiful; pathetic

2. YLSUGURULOBI = 2. LUGUBRIOUSLY
Mournfully; gloomily

3. ERNLKA = 3. RANKLE
Irritate or cause resentment

4. EIATPRRN = 4. TERRAPIN
North American aquatic turtle

5. FEUEBLDDD = 5. BEFUDDLED
Puzzled; perplexed

6. OINSDSLUE = 6. DELUSIONS
False beliefs or opinions

7. UFTELI = 7. FUTILE
Hopeless

8. TERSPTOIENU = 8. PRETENTIOUS
Puffed-up; self-important

9. GILEYNGR = 9. GINGERLY
Carefully

10. XEEEDTPARAS = 10. EXASPERATED
Angered or greatly annoyed

11. UOONISM = 11. OMINOUS
Threatening

12. ILUEAVVDLE = 12. VAUDEVILLE
Stage act

13. BINGOIGL = 13. OBLIGING
Helpful

14. PIEADIDTLDA = 14. DILAPIDATED
Shabby; neglected

15. NAGEDLOTEI = 15. DELEGATION
Assigned group

Jacob Vocabulary Juggle Letters 3

1. REVEFNT = 1. _____
   Having great emotion or zeal

2. ENTIARRP = 2. _____
   North American aquatic turtle

3. NSRUEOIETTP = 3. _____
   Puffed-up; self-important

4. RSPNALEH = 4. _____
   Shell fragments from an explosion

5. ETSEOMNARCRN = 5. _____
   Objection; protest

6. XTSEAAPREED = 6. _____
   Angered or greatly annoyed

7. UROUYBGUISLL = 7. _____
   Mournfully; gloomily

8. LTPAUTEN = 8. _____
   Irritable or ill-tempered

9. BNOIIGGL = 9. _____
   Helpful

10. TTOCPEMN =10. _____
    Dislike

11. IGRLEYGN =11. _____
    Carefully

12. OESUD =12. _____
    Put out; extinguish

13. ADEUIVLEVL =13. _____
    Stage act

14. DDNESHMIII =14. _____
    Made smaller; lessened

15. MLSAAHECRK =15. _____
    Falling to ruin; tumbled-down

Copyrighted

Jacob Vocabulary Juggle Letters 3 Answer Key

1. REVEFNT = 1. FERVENT
Having great emotion or zeal

2. ENTIARRP = 2. TERRAPIN
North American aquatic turtle

3. NSRUEOIETTP = 3. PRETENTIOUS
Puffed-up; self-important

4. RSPNALEH = 4. SHRAPNEL
Shell fragments from an explosion

5. ETSEOMNARCRN = 5. REMONSTRANCE
Objection; protest

6. XTSEAAPREED = 6. EXASPERATED
Angered or greatly annoyed

7. UROUYBGUISLL = 7. LUGUBRIOUSLY
Mournfully; gloomily

8. LTPAUTEN = 8. PETULANT
Irritable or ill-tempered

9. BNOIIGGL = 9. OBLIGING
Helpful

10. TTOCPEMN =10. CONTEMPT
Dislike

11. IGRLEYGN =11. GINGERLY
Carefully

12. OESUD =12. DOUSE
Put out; extinguish

13. ADEUIVLEVL =13. VAUDEVILLE
Stage act

14. DDNESHMIII =14. DIMINISHED
Made smaller; lessened

15. MLSAAHECRK =15. RAMSHACKLE
Falling to ruin; tumbled-down

Jacob Vocabulary Juggle Letters 4

1. DHSRSA = 1. _____
   Fragments of a brittle substance, as of glass or metal

2. UIEOTSP = 2. _____
   Pitiful; pathetic

3. OIFMSTCEDID = 3. _____
   Frustrated

4. UATDNEUND = 4. _____
   Not discouraged or disheartened

5. DCLEOJA = 5. _____
   Urged; appealed

6. ERRMNNASTCOE = 6. _____
   Objection; protest

7. PEXSAREEDTA = 7. _____
   Angered or greatly annoyed

8. IUNOMOS = 8. _____
   Threatening

9. TRORIBNSAEA = 9. _____
   Quirks; abnormalities

10. UPEETINSTRO = 10. _____
    Puffed-up; self-important

11. YTLLNONBEVEE = 11. _____
    Kindly

12. LIEVELDAVU = 12. _____
    Stage act

13. GIILNOBG = 13. _____
    Helpful

14. ARUTESOB = 14. _____
    One who undermines

15. EUPOCIASRR = 15. _____
    Dangerously insecure; unstable

Jacob Vocabulary Juggle Letters 4 Answer Key

1. DHSRSA = 1. SHARDS
Fragments of a brittle substance, as of glass or metal

2. UIEOTSP = 2. PITEOUS
Pitiful; pathetic

3. OIFMSTCEDID = 3. DISCOMFITED
Frustrated

4. UATDNEUND = 4. UNDAUNTED
Not discouraged or disheartened

5. DCLEOJA = 5. CAJOLED
Urged; appealed

6. ERRMNNASTCOE = 6. REMONSTRANCE
Objection; protest

7. PEXSAREEDTA = 7. EXASPERATED
Angered or greatly annoyed

8. IUNOMOS = 8. OMINOUS
Threatening

9. TRORIBNSAEA = 9. ABERRATIONS
Quirks; abnormalities

10. UPEETINSTRO = 10. PRETENTIOUS
Puffed-up; self-important

11. YTLLNONBEVEE = 11. BENEVOLENTLY
Kindly

12. LIEVELDAVU = 12. VAUDEVILLE
Stage act

13. GIILNOBG = 13. OBLIGING
Helpful

14. ARUTESOB = 14. SABOTEUR
One who undermines

15. EUPOCIASRR = 15. PRECARIOUS
Dangerously insecure; unstable

ABERRATIONS	Quirks; abnormalities
BEFUDDLED	Puzzled; perplexed
BENEVOLENTLY	Kindly
CAJOLED	Urged; appealed
CONTEMPT	Dislike
DELEGATION	Assigned group
DELUSIONS	False beliefs or opinions

DILAPIDATED	Shabby; neglected
DIMINISHED	Made smaller; lessened
DISCOMFITED	Frustrated
DOUSE	Put out; extinguish
EXASPERATED	Angered or greatly annoyed
EXULTATION	Great joy
FELLED	Chopped

FERVENT	Having great emotion or zeal
FICKLE	Changeable
FUTILE	Hopeless
GINGERLY	Carefully
IRONY	Contrast; incongruity
LITANY	Series of prayers
LUGUBRIOUSLY	Mournfully; gloomily

LYRICIST	One who writes words to songs
MACHINATIONS	Schemes; plots
MELANCHOLY	Sadness
OBLIGING	Helpful
OMINOUS	Threatening
PARAGORIC	Opium form taken to relieve intestinal pain
PETULANT	Irritable or ill-tempered

PITEOUS	Pitiful; pathetic
PRECARIOUS	Dangerously insecure; unstable
PRETENTIOUS	Puffed-up; self-important
RAMSHACKLE	Falling to ruin; tumbled-down
RANKLE	Irritate or cause resentment
REFURBISHED	Refinished
REMONSTRANCE	Objection; protest

RIVULET	Small stream
SABOTEUR	One who undermines
SHARDS	Fragments of a brittle substance, as of glass or metal
SHRAPNEL	Shell fragments from an explosion
TERRAPIN	North American aquatic turtle
TORRENT	Flood; overflow
TREACHEROUS	Extremely unsafe

UNDAUNTED	Not discouraged or disheartened
VAUDEVILLE	Stage act

Jacob Vocabulary

RANKLE	VAUDEVILLE	DELUSIONS	SHARDS	OMINOUS
DIMINISHED	IRONY	SHRAPNEL	TERRAPIN	BEFUDDLED
GINGERLY	PRECARIOUS	FREE SPACE	CONTEMPT	DISCOMFITED
MELANCHOLY	DILAPIDATED	CAJOLED	REMONSTRANCE	FICKLE
BENEVOLENTLY	EXASPERATED	LUGUBRIOUSLY	FUTILE	TORRENT

Jacob Vocabulary

PRETENTIOUS	FELLED	RIVULET	LYRICIST	ABERRATIONS
PETULANT	TREACHEROUS	DOUSE	PITEOUS	MACHINATIONS
EXULTATION	DELEGATION	FREE SPACE	REFURBISHED	PARAGORIC
LITANY	OBLIGING	FERVENT	UNDAUNTED	TORRENT
FUTILE	LUGUBRIOUSLY	EXASPERATED	BENEVOLENTLY	FICKLE

Jacob Vocabulary

VAUDEVILLE	CONTEMPT	OMINOUS	SHRAPNEL	GINGERLY
TERRAPIN	BEFUDDLED	SHARDS	PARAGORIC	CAJOLED
PETULANT	BENEVOLENTLY	FREE SPACE	MELANCHOLY	MACHINATIONS
DELEGATION	FUTILE	IRONY	DIMINISHED	RAMSHACKLE
LYRICIST	RIVULET	REMONSTRANCE	ABERRATIONS	LUGUBRIOUSLY

Jacob Vocabulary

PRECARIOUS	PITEOUS	UNDAUNTED	EXULTATION	OBLIGING
TREACHEROUS	FELLED	TORRENT	DISCOMFITED	FERVENT
DELUSIONS	FICKLE	FREE SPACE	SABOTEUR	PRETENTIOUS
REFURBISHED	DILAPIDATED	RANKLE	LITANY	LUGUBRIOUSLY
ABERRATIONS	REMONSTRANCE	RIVULET	LYRICIST	RAMSHACKLE

Jacob Vocabulary

BEFUDDLED	CAJOLED	EXASPERATED	RIVULET	PRECARIOUS
DELUSIONS	DILAPIDATED	UNDAUNTED	LYRICIST	PETULANT
EXULTATION	FELLED	FREE SPACE	MELANCHOLY	OMINOUS
CONTEMPT	REFURBISHED	TERRAPIN	FERVENT	TORRENT
FUTILE	LITANY	VAUDEVILLE	IRONY	PITEOUS

Jacob Vocabulary

OBLIGING	GINGERLY	BENEVOLENTLY	MACHINATIONS	FICKLE
SHRAPNEL	DOUSE	SHARDS	SABOTEUR	PRETENTIOUS
PARAGORIC	ABERRATIONS	FREE SPACE	DISCOMFITED	LUGUBRIOUSLY
REMONSTRANCE	RANKLE	TREACHEROUS	DIMINISHED	PITEOUS
IRONY	VAUDEVILLE	LITANY	FUTILE	TORRENT

Jacob Vocabulary

TORRENT	GINGERLY	VAUDEVILLE	DISCOMFITED	FELLED
LUGUBRIOUSLY	DILAPIDATED	IRONY	SHRAPNEL	LYRICIST
RANKLE	SABOTEUR	FREE SPACE	ABERRATIONS	FERVENT
FICKLE	LITANY	CONTEMPT	PETULANT	TREACHEROUS
RAMSHACKLE	FUTILE	BEFUDDLED	PITEOUS	EXASPERATED

Jacob Vocabulary

TERRAPIN	DIMINISHED	UNDAUNTED	REMONSTRANCE	SHARDS
OBLIGING	PARAGORIC	BENEVOLENTLY	MACHINATIONS	PRETENTIOUS
OMINOUS	RIVULET	FREE SPACE	DELUSIONS	DELEGATION
DOUSE	CAJOLED	MELANCHOLY	EXULTATION	EXASPERATED
PITEOUS	BEFUDDLED	FUTILE	RAMSHACKLE	TREACHEROUS

Jacob Vocabulary

VAUDEVILLE	MELANCHOLY	PRECARIOUS	SHRAPNEL	RANKLE
FICKLE	CONTEMPT	PITEOUS	PRETENTIOUS	GINGERLY
PETULANT	DELEGATION	FREE SPACE	LITANY	TREACHEROUS
REMONSTRANCE	EXULTATION	FUTILE	UNDAUNTED	LYRICIST
SABOTEUR	RAMSHACKLE	PARAGORIC	DELUSIONS	FELLED

Jacob Vocabulary

TORRENT	DIMINISHED	ABERRATIONS	IRONY	DOUSE
RIVULET	REFURBISHED	TERRAPIN	LUGUBRIOUSLY	BENEVOLENTLY
BEFUDDLED	SHARDS	FREE SPACE	CAJOLED	DISCOMFITED
EXASPERATED	MACHINATIONS	DILAPIDATED	FERVENT	FELLED
DELUSIONS	PARAGORIC	RAMSHACKLE	SABOTEUR	LYRICIST

Jacob Vocabulary

PARAGORIC	LUGUBRIOUSLY	EXASPERATED	IRONY	MACHINATIONS
MELANCHOLY	REMONSTRANCE	OMINOUS	PITEOUS	DIMINISHED
RAMSHACKLE	TERRAPIN	FREE SPACE	REFURBISHED	TREACHEROUS
TORRENT	RANKLE	DOUSE	RIVULET	BEFUDDLED
DILAPIDATED	DELEGATION	SHRAPNEL	UNDAUNTED	DELUSIONS

Jacob Vocabulary

SABOTEUR	EXULTATION	LITANY	FERVENT	FICKLE
PRECARIOUS	ABERRATIONS	FELLED	GINGERLY	PETULANT
OBLIGING	SHARDS	FREE SPACE	CAJOLED	CONTEMPT
BENEVOLENTLY	VAUDEVILLE	DISCOMFITED	LYRICIST	DELUSIONS
UNDAUNTED	SHRAPNEL	DELEGATION	DILAPIDATED	BEFUDDLED

Jacob Vocabulary

SABOTEUR	FUTILE	TREACHEROUS	PETULANT	IRONY
REFURBISHED	DELUSIONS	LITANY	FELLED	CAJOLED
DOUSE	DILAPIDATED	FREE SPACE	VAUDEVILLE	RIVULET
UNDAUNTED	LYRICIST	RAMSHACKLE	OBLIGING	DISCOMFITED
TORRENT	BEFUDDLED	FERVENT	SHARDS	CONTEMPT

Jacob Vocabulary

RANKLE	FICKLE	DELEGATION	EXASPERATED	PITEOUS
GINGERLY	EXULTATION	BENEVOLENTLY	PARAGORIC	OMINOUS
SHRAPNEL	REMONSTRANCE	FREE SPACE	TERRAPIN	ABERRATIONS
PRETENTIOUS	DIMINISHED	LUGUBRIOUSLY	PRECARIOUS	CONTEMPT
SHARDS	FERVENT	BEFUDDLED	TORRENT	DISCOMFITED

Jacob Vocabulary

SHARDS	DIMINISHED	PRETENTIOUS	BENEVOLENTLY	REMONSTRANCE
MACHINATIONS	DELEGATION	REFURBISHED	FERVENT	OBLIGING
FUTILE	TORRENT	FREE SPACE	OMINOUS	ABERRATIONS
RIVULET	MELANCHOLY	LITANY	IRONY	SABOTEUR
PARAGORIC	BEFUDDLED	RANKLE	DELUSIONS	TREACHEROUS

Jacob Vocabulary

PITEOUS	CAJOLED	VAUDEVILLE	PETULANT	LUGUBRIOUSLY
CONTEMPT	LYRICIST	DISCOMFITED	DILAPIDATED	FICKLE
FELLED	UNDAUNTED	FREE SPACE	RAMSHACKLE	EXULTATION
EXASPERATED	PRECARIOUS	SHRAPNEL	GINGERLY	TREACHEROUS
DELUSIONS	RANKLE	BEFUDDLED	PARAGORIC	SABOTEUR

Jacob Vocabulary

PARAGORIC	GINGERLY	MACHINATIONS	TREACHEROUS	FELLED
BENEVOLENTLY	PETULANT	UNDAUNTED	RANKLE	IRONY
EXULTATION	CONTEMPT	FREE SPACE	SHRAPNEL	DOUSE
RIVULET	OBLIGING	FUTILE	BEFUDDLED	RAMSHACKLE
CAJOLED	VAUDEVILLE	LITANY	OMINOUS	TERRAPIN

Jacob Vocabulary

EXASPERATED	MELANCHOLY	FICKLE	TORRENT	DISCOMFITED
PITEOUS	REMONSTRANCE	ABERRATIONS	DELUSIONS	PRECARIOUS
SABOTEUR	LUGUBRIOUSLY	FREE SPACE	REFURBISHED	FERVENT
DELEGATION	LYRICIST	DIMINISHED	DILAPIDATED	TERRAPIN
OMINOUS	LITANY	VAUDEVILLE	CAJOLED	RAMSHACKLE

Jacob Vocabulary

FELLED	DELUSIONS	LYRICIST	PARAGORIC	ABERRATIONS
GINGERLY	PETULANT	SHARDS	TORRENT	FERVENT
BEFUDDLED	RANKLE	FREE SPACE	MELANCHOLY	UNDAUNTED
PITEOUS	RAMSHACKLE	TERRAPIN	SHRAPNEL	FICKLE
DISCOMFITED	TREACHEROUS	LITANY	REFURBISHED	FUTILE

Jacob Vocabulary

RIVULET	EXASPERATED	PRECARIOUS	OMINOUS	DOUSE
REMONSTRANCE	DILAPIDATED	DIMINISHED	LUGUBRIOUSLY	IRONY
CONTEMPT	MACHINATIONS	FREE SPACE	VAUDEVILLE	CAJOLED
DELEGATION	SABOTEUR	BENEVOLENTLY	PRETENTIOUS	FUTILE
REFURBISHED	LITANY	TREACHEROUS	DISCOMFITED	FICKLE

Jacob Vocabulary

CONTEMPT	TERRAPIN	BENEVOLENTLY	PRECARIOUS	FICKLE
REFURBISHED	LUGUBRIOUSLY	RAMSHACKLE	REMONSTRANCE	RIVULET
PETULANT	SHRAPNEL	FREE SPACE	OMINOUS	DIMINISHED
PARAGORIC	UNDAUNTED	TORRENT	IRONY	DELUSIONS
SHARDS	MELANCHOLY	EXASPERATED	GINGERLY	DISCOMFITED

Jacob Vocabulary

VAUDEVILLE	SABOTEUR	DELEGATION	PRETENTIOUS	CAJOLED
EXULTATION	FERVENT	MACHINATIONS	OBLIGING	RANKLE
DOUSE	FUTILE	FREE SPACE	LYRICIST	BEFUDDLED
ABERRATIONS	LITANY	PITEOUS	FELLED	DISCOMFITED
GINGERLY	EXASPERATED	MELANCHOLY	SHARDS	DELUSIONS

Jacob Vocabulary

FELLED	REMONSTRANCE	PRETENTIOUS	IRONY	GINGERLY
DISCOMFITED	PARAGORIC	EXASPERATED	MACHINATIONS	PRECARIOUS
FUTILE	OBLIGING	FREE SPACE	FERVENT	SABOTEUR
EXULTATION	LUGUBRIOUSLY	FICKLE	DELEGATION	REFURBISHED
PITEOUS	SHARDS	VAUDEVILLE	TREACHEROUS	RAMSHACKLE

Jacob Vocabulary

MELANCHOLY	PETULANT	LYRICIST	LITANY	DOUSE
RIVULET	TERRAPIN	TORRENT	DIMINISHED	BEFUDDLED
CONTEMPT	BENEVOLENTLY	FREE SPACE	RANKLE	DILAPIDATED
SHRAPNEL	ABERRATIONS	CAJOLED	UNDAUNTED	RAMSHACKLE
TREACHEROUS	VAUDEVILLE	SHARDS	PITEOUS	REFURBISHED

Jacob Vocabulary

REMONSTRANCE	OMINOUS	FUTILE	PETULANT	GINGERLY
FICKLE	SHARDS	TERRAPIN	FERVENT	SHRAPNEL
DILAPIDATED	IRONY	FREE SPACE	OBLIGING	LITANY
DISCOMFITED	PARAGORIC	DOUSE	DIMINISHED	RIVULET
EXASPERATED	LYRICIST	CONTEMPT	VAUDEVILLE	DELEGATION

Jacob Vocabulary

BEFUDDLED	PITEOUS	FELLED	PRECARIOUS	BENEVOLENTLY
PRETENTIOUS	RAMSHACKLE	MELANCHOLY	TREACHEROUS	ABERRATIONS
LUGUBRIOUSLY	TORRENT	FREE SPACE	CAJOLED	EXULTATION
REFURBISHED	SABOTEUR	MACHINATIONS	DELUSIONS	DELEGATION
VAUDEVILLE	CONTEMPT	LYRICIST	EXASPERATED	RIVULET

Jacob Vocabulary

TERRAPIN	OMINOUS	LUGUBRIOUSLY	DELEGATION	IRONY
MELANCHOLY	TORRENT	SHARDS	PRETENTIOUS	PETULANT
RAMSHACKLE	DELUSIONS	FREE SPACE	EXASPERATED	FUTILE
CONTEMPT	PRECARIOUS	PITEOUS	RIVULET	VAUDEVILLE
REFURBISHED	CAJOLED	LITANY	SHRAPNEL	PARAGORIC

Jacob Vocabulary

FELLED	MACHINATIONS	REMONSTRANCE	ABERRATIONS	DOUSE
DILAPIDATED	LYRICIST	BENEVOLENTLY	RANKLE	FICKLE
DISCOMFITED	UNDAUNTED	FREE SPACE	DIMINISHED	TREACHEROUS
EXULTATION	BEFUDDLED	GINGERLY	SABOTEUR	PARAGORIC
SHRAPNEL	LITANY	CAJOLED	REFURBISHED	VAUDEVILLE

Jacob Vocabulary

FELLED	RANKLE	OMINOUS	OBLIGING	REFURBISHED
GINGERLY	SHRAPNEL	FUTILE	ABERRATIONS	FICKLE
TREACHEROUS	REMONSTRANCE	FREE SPACE	BEFUDDLED	IRONY
PITEOUS	TORRENT	CONTEMPT	DISCOMFITED	UNDAUNTED
DIMINISHED	RIVULET	LYRICIST	VAUDEVILLE	EXULTATION

Jacob Vocabulary

DOUSE	PARAGORIC	LITANY	DELUSIONS	SHARDS
MELANCHOLY	PRETENTIOUS	TERRAPIN	EXASPERATED	BENEVOLENTLY
DILAPIDATED	DELEGATION	FREE SPACE	RAMSHACKLE	LUGUBRIOUSLY
FERVENT	SABOTEUR	CAJOLED	PRECARIOUS	EXULTATION
VAUDEVILLE	LYRICIST	RIVULET	DIMINISHED	UNDAUNTED

Jacob Vocabulary

CONTEMPT	TERRAPIN	PRETENTIOUS	CAJOLED	PRECARIOUS
DIMINISHED	RANKLE	FUTILE	REMONSTRANCE	GINGERLY
LITANY	TORRENT	FREE SPACE	OBLIGING	TREACHEROUS
FERVENT	DOUSE	IRONY	OMINOUS	LYRICIST
ABERRATIONS	MACHINATIONS	BEFUDDLED	DELUSIONS	EXULTATION

Jacob Vocabulary

SHRAPNEL	DILAPIDATED	PETULANT	REFURBISHED	FELLED
UNDAUNTED	FICKLE	DISCOMFITED	BENEVOLENTLY	DELEGATION
MELANCHOLY	PITEOUS	FREE SPACE	SHARDS	VAUDEVILLE
SABOTEUR	PARAGORIC	RIVULET	LUGUBRIOUSLY	EXULTATION
DELUSIONS	BEFUDDLED	MACHINATIONS	ABERRATIONS	LYRICIST

www.ingramcontent.com/pod-product-compliance
Lightning Source LLC
Chambersburg PA
CBHW081457070526
44586CB00019B/2389